DECISIONS AT 13/14+

Also by Michael Smith
and Veronica Matthew

Decisions at 15/16+

Decisions at 17/18+

Decisions at 13/14+

The starting point for GCSE options

Michael Smith
Headmaster,
Filton High School, Bristol
County of Avon

Veronica Matthew
Senior Lecturer in Law
De Montfort University
Leicester

CRAC

HOBSONS

1st National Curriculum Edition

Acknowledgments
The authors wish to express their thanks to the following for
their assistance:
Cornhill Insurance; all employers; examination groups;
professional bodies; the Leicestershire Careers Service
Information Unit, City Careers Centre, Pocklingtons Walk,
Leicester, and regional councils for further education who have
supplied information; John Laing, Kit Tyrell and Sue Smith. Peter
Dines, sometime Deputy Chief Executive of the Secondary
Examinations Council; and Principals of that Council for
information on GCSE. The Controller of Her Majesty's
Stationery Office; The Training Commission – Youth Training
News; John Taylor and Tim Cornford of the National
Curriculum Council; Paddy Radcliffe, Head of Careers at The
Manor Community College, Cambridge; Louisa Prentis and her
parents, and Mr F Murphy at The Manor Community College.

Note
Any reference to a person of one sex in this publication is to be
taken as including a reference to the other sex, unless otherwise
specified. No attempt has been made to give special consideration
to Scottish school-leaving qualifications.

ISBN 1 85324 660 3

© 1976, 1980, 1983, 1985, 1988, 1993 Hobsons
Publishing PLC, Bateman Street, Cambridge CB2 1LZ
First published 1972 by the Careers Research and
Advisory Centre
Second edition 1976, Hobsons Publishing PLC
Bateman Street, Cambridge CB2 1LZ
Reprinted 1977, 1978, 1979 (twice)
Third edition 1980, Hobsons Publishing PLC
Reprinted 1981, 1982 (twice)
Fourth edition 1983
Reprinted 1984 with new cover design and new series title
Decisions
Fifth edition 1985
Reprinted 1986
Sixth edition 1988
Reprinted 1989, 1990.
Revised 1993 with new cover design and new series title *Student
Helpbooks*

CRAC

The Careers Research and Advisory Centre is a registered
educational charity. Hobsons Publishing PLC produces CRAC
publications under exclusive licence and royalty agreements.

Cover artwork by Amanda Hall
Text illustrations by John Riley
Printed in England by Clays Ltd, St Ives plc
Ref. L076/i10qq/A/JC

It's Your Choice

Careers Guide

An A~Z description of careers from Accountancy to Zookeeping

Each entry includes:

☛ Required qualifications

☛ Details of further reading

☛ Who to contact for more information

Pages 160~317

1

It's Your Choice

1 **Ready to Jump?**

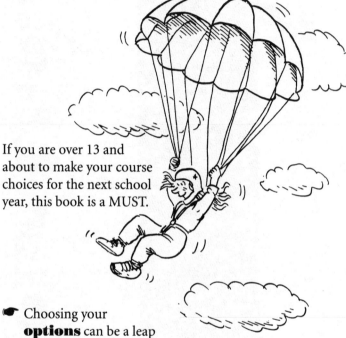

If you are over 13 and about to make your course choices for the next school year, this book is a MUST.

- ☛ Choosing your **options** can be a leap in the dark or a controlled jump where you know just where you are going.
- ☛ **GCSE** (General Certificate of Secondary Education) is ahead of you.
- ☛ **Career** requirements must be explored or you could miss out in the future.

This book aims to help you to get it right. You need to think your way through some rather important questions.

How are sensible decisions made?

What does it mean to study a particular subject?

What will be tested at the end of the course?

How will the testing be organised?

What do the GCSE grades mean?

How do GCSE grades match National Curriculum attainment targets?

Which subjects must I include?

Which subjects should I choose?

Which subjects should I leave out?

How do I make my choice?

These are vital questions. They all demand an answer. Get them wrong and you could find yourself in difficulties. Get them right and the two years 14 to 16 could be the best springboard you ever landed on.

2 Making Decisions

This may be the first time you have been asked to make a decision which will affect your future. That may sound forbidding but you had better get used to the idea, for there are a whole series of them lurking around the corner.

D for Decision

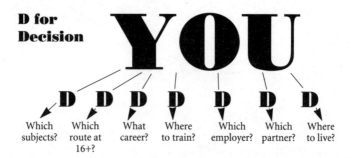

YOU

D	D	D	D	D	D	D
Which subjects?	Which route at 16+?	What career?	Where to train?	Which employer?	Which partner?	Where to live?

Now   **The Mid-1990s and Beyond**

These decisions are important for they will affect your life style which includes friends, holidays, bank balance, leisure interests and a whole range of satisfactions. They all connect together.

Putting it this way makes it look automatic. But this is far from the case. The whole game is more like snakes and ladders. Above are the ladders – we've done away with the snakes. Take a look in the diary and see if you can find some.

Diary of a disaster about to happen

Extracts from David's Diary

1992 January

Some great things about school this year. PE for a start. I'm in the Year 9 school soccer squad. There's a new teacher for science. Sue says he's horrible.

1992 March

Course choices for two years – that's donkey's years. I'm not looking forward to more science. Sue was right. Wish there was a GCSE in football. Old Smithy asked me today what I was doing for a career. How would I know? I think I'll just take single integrated science. I wonder what my mates are doing?

1994 August

Great week, GCSE results – 2Cs, 3Ds, 1F, 1G and a training place in Cooksons' Kitchens.

1995 July

Cooksons' have offered me a permanent place in the kitchens. I was one of the lucky ones. Boss said I could be a manager if I took more exams. Wonder if I would pass them?

1995 August

Catering is OK. Better get on one of those advanced courses at the Tech. More qualifications mean more cash and that means better holidays. Just the job!

1995 Sept

Got a letter from Loamshire Tech. Did not have at least two grade Cs in double science, so they won't have me. Why don't they tell you these things? That's my promotion gone for a start.

1996 May

Can't get any further with this job. I'm stuck. Wonder if Mary's outfit has any jobs down the works. Careers Office might have something. <u>If only I'd got things straight earlier.</u>

Talking Point

Can you spot the mistakes which David made between January 1992 and May 1996?

Five logical steps to make a decision

Below is a series of steps which, if you take them slowly, get your facts straight and take plenty of advice, should help you to come to a compromise solution. Remember you are not searching for *one* right answer. You are looking for one sensible answer among several.

1 **Get the question clear.**
What are you being asked?
What are the alternatives?
How important are they?

2 **Find out the facts.**
What do you need to know?
What are the facts?
Where can you obtain them?

3 **Weigh them up.**
Which facts matter most?
Which facts matter least?
Where do they lead?

4 **Make the decision.**
Which aspects come first
What is the heart of the problem?
What follows?

5 **Check results.**
Does the decision look right?
Does the decision feel right?
When can changes come if needed?

Where shall we go for our holidays?

1

Get the question clear.
What do we all want from it?
Hotel or self-catering?
One place or moving around?
Inland or by the sea?

2

Find out the facts.
What do the travel firms offer?
How much do they charge?
What do the brochures say?
Who has been there and can tell us?

3

Weigh them up.
What are the important aspects?
What does not matter much?
Which is the most attractive?
Which has most to offer?

4

Make the decision.
When must it be made?
Have we thought of everything?
Can we afford it?
Is everyone happy with it?

5

Check results.
Did we enjoy the holiday?
Did it give all it promised?
Did we spend too much?
Would you recommend it?

Which subjects shall I choose?

1

Get the question clear.
What decisions have to be made?
Which subjects lead to exams?
How long have I to choose?
What's around to help me?

2

Find out the facts.
What subject skills do I need?
Are there new subjects?
What are my strengths?
What are my weaknesses?

3

Weigh them up.
What will I need for my career?
What if my career changes?
Is dropping subjects dangerous?
How can I get a balance?

4

Make the decision.
Has everyone been consulted?
Is this my own choice?
Am I happy with it?
Are there any doubts left over?

5

Check results.
Wait until the course starts
Give each subject a fair trial
Get advice if unhappy
Don't leave it too long

3 Why Must I Choose?

Forty years ago there was no choice. The old School Certificate (the examination which existed even before O-levels) was just a pass/fail test with a set range of subjects. This may have been fine for the 1940s but it will not do for the 1990s and beyond to the twenty-first century. The world has moved on. The frontiers of knowledge have been pushed out. There is now more to know.

Some topics which could not have appeared in an examination course 40 years ago:

English	Writings of Boris Pasternak, John Osborne, Alan Sillitoe
Mathematics	Computer studies
History	The Cold War, conservation, carbon-dating
Geography	Nuclear power, North Sea gas, satellite weather forecasting
Biology	The electron microscope, structure of the cell, DNA
Chemistry	Polymer technology, radioactivity
Physics	The transistor, the microprocessor
Design studies	Plastics technology
Home economics	Microwave cookery
Music	The Beatles, Benjamin Britten
Drama	*The Caretaker, Guys and Dolls, Oliver*

To discover why there is choice, take a look at Fred – who is obviously in difficulties:

There are 3 problems lurking here

Time
Fred is trying to
beat the clock
Talents
with too much
on his plate
Choice
without it Fred
is unhappy

Translate this into Years 10 and 11 courses and the
reasons for choice become clear.

Time

Knowledge has extended to such a degree in so many
subjects that there is not enough time between now and
16 to study the whole range in sufficient depth. So, we
choose.

Talents

No one is good at everything, but each of us can be good
at something. If we study our best subjects in depth we
will improve our skills in them. So, we choose.

Choice

Personal likes and dislikes become more pronounced as
we grow older. By 14 our choices become more closely
linked to how well we get on with our subjects. So we
choose.

4 Getting a Balance

Climbed any mountains lately? One of the difficult aspects of preparing for outdoor pursuits is deciding what kit to take before starting out on an expedition. Too little will leave you unprepared for emergencies. Too much will weigh you down so that you can't cover the ground. If you expect one sort of weather conditions you may be unprepared for another.

What will you take?

Tents with sewn-in groundsheets
Ropes
Compasses
Bootlaces
Stretchers
Whistles
Transistor radios
Maps
Emergency rations
Crampons
Skis
Goggles
Dustbin liners
Boots
Anoraks
Sweaters
First-aid kits
Food
Hurricane lamps
Rucksacks
Mackintoshes
Stoves and fuel

Woollen shirts
Spare clothes
Extra woollen socks
Woollen trousers
Jeans
Gloves
Water containers
Matches
Sleeping bags
Blankets
Sunglasses
Flares
Climbing harnesses
Ice axes
Splints
Torches
Oxygen
Alarm clocks
Plastic bags
Route cards
Waterproofs
Suitcases
Survival bags

You Choose

The expedition is a two-day ascent in June of a 3,000-foot mountain. Ten miles are to be covered each day. Camp is at 1,200 feet. The weather forecast promises sun and rain. What gear would you take to achieve a balance of comfort, enjoyment and safety?

For the answer see page 152.

There is a curious feature in this kind of decision-making. Because you cannot accurately predict weather conditions, accidents, personalities, timing and gradients, you have to take a balanced range of resources to meet most known hazards. But when you come down the mountain and reach your base, you will know precisely what you should have taken.

There is a strong parallel with subjects available for GCSE.

Subject Choice

English	French	Design and
Mathematics	German	Technology
Physics	History	Religious
Chemistry	Geography	Education
Biology	Business Studies	Music
Single Science	Art	Physical
Double Science	Food Technology	Education

How do you know what you will need? Let us look at the situation.

Examine the things you know

1 You will – you hope – choose a career.
2 You know your strong subjects.
3 You know your weak subjects.
4 You know that results are important.
5 You know how well you work.
6 You know how you respond to a challenge.

Examine the things you do not know

1 You do not know which career it will be.
2 You cannot know the precise demands it will make.
3 You do not know how you or it will change.
4 You cannot predict changes in qualifications needed.
5 You cannot foresee your personal circumstances.
6 You do not know how technology may develop.

Choosing subjects against a range of knowns and unknowns is not easy. Just as in the mountain expedition, you need to ensure a

Each of the main subjects areas will be useful to you at some time in the future. Think of each as a weight on a seesaw. Line up your weights so they balance.

What Does Each of These Subject Areas Have to Offer?

English

We cannot get far without words. They enable us to communicate. Most of the information we receive is passed on in words. When you have mastered the language you have a powerful tool at your disposal. The study of literature can be a most enriching experience. It should be an absolute essential for everyone.

Mathematics

More symbols. They enable us to make generalisations from exact data and are particularly helpful in solving real problems from models. They help us to recognise patterns and relationships and come to logical conclusions. This is not an area to fear. You probably know more mathematics than you think. Another 'must' for everybody.

Modern Languages

When you can speak a foreign language you have an introduction to people whose speech, customs and culture are different from your own. International relationships have never been more important in economic, political and cultural terms. How can you sell anything to a country if you can't speak its language? From a career point of view, people who can speak another European language will be particularly useful. Most people believe this is another essential for all, now that Britain is a member of the European Community.

Science

Scientists ask questions and in order to find the answers, set up experiments and observe. The results, which are recorded accurately, help them to come to conclusions. You live in a technological world and without some scientific knowledge you will not be well enough equipped to understand it. So in one form or another, it is another 'must' for all.

Humanities

If you are curious about the world around you, about people and places, past and present, then these subjects (history, geography, religious education, etc) are for you. The skills and knowledge that you gain when you study the humanities will be very rewarding and many employers regard them highly when interviewing people for jobs.

Creative Subjects

Whatever the medium - drama, art or music - creative work can be intensely satisfying. To explore form and space, colour and sound, material and matter involves a whole variety of skills which are valuable for both work and leisure. They can also help you earn your living – if you are good at them.

Technological Subjects

The applications of scientific ideas is at the core of good design. Business, industry and individual consumers alike rely heavily on well-designed, reliable technology. No one whose working career will span the twenty-first century will be properly equipped without a soundly based experience of its fundamentals.

What About New Subjects Not Offered Before?

Many schools offer subjects in Years 10 and 11 that you will not have met before. These may make choice difficult but they often have important career significance.

Computer studies	This involves understanding logical thought processes, and the impact of computers and microprocessors on society.
Economics	This is a theoretically based subject, which studies the principles of money, trade, industry and financial processes.
Sociology	A people-based study concerned largely with groups of human beings and how they behave and interact with each other.
Keyboard skills	Basic skills which are very useful for those entering the secretarial world as well as for increasing personal competence in using computers for all careers.
Accounts/ Business Studies	An introductory course on commerce and financial control, providing another good insight into the business world.

What To Aim For

In the end your choice will be a personal one – but
wherever you are at school, whatever you are inclined
towards and however many subjects you include, make
absolutely sure that it is **balanced**.

**English
Mathematics
A foreign language
A science
One of the humanities
A creative subject
A technological subject**

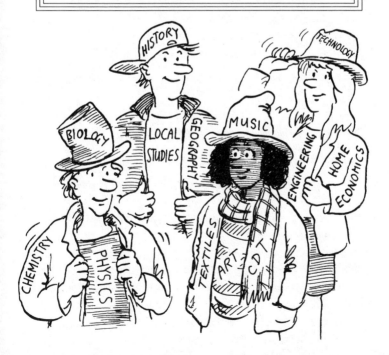

How The National Curriculum Helps You to Get This Balance

The National Curriculum was first introduced into schools in 1989. This means that every state school run by a local education authority or grant maintained school run by central government has to provide a basic curriculum consisting of religious education and subjects of the National Curriculum up to the end of Year 11.

To quote the law:

… schools must provide a balanced and broadly based curriculum which

☞ Promotes the spiritual, moral and cultural, mental and physical development of pupils at school and of society

☞ prepares pupils for the opportunities, responsibilities and experiences of adult life

from the 1988 Education Act

Why Have a National Curriculum?

The National Curriculum Council states that the National Curriculum will provide:

☞ **Your teachers** with clear objectives for their teaching

☞ **You** with identifiable targets to aim for

☞ **Your parents** with accurate information about what you can be expected to know, understand and be able to do

☞ **Your future employers** with information about what you have actually achieved.

The overall result should mean that you have higher expectations and more effective progression throughout the years of full-time education, at the end of which you should be better prepared for life and work.

What Subjects Appear in the National Curriculum?

You will hear people refer to **Core** and **Foundation** subjects. All ten subjects which feature in the National Curriculum are foundation subjects but three of them

English
Science
Mathematics

are described as core subjects and were the first to be introduced. **Up to the end of Key Stage 3** (ie up to end of Year 9) the picture looked like this:

As well as religious education, the following had to be taught

Core	Foundation
Mathematics	History
English	Geography
Science	Technology
Welsh*	Music
	Art
	A modern foreign language
	Physical education
	Welsh*

* In Wales, Welsh will be a core subject in schools where it is the language every subject is taught in; in the remaining schools, it will be a foundation subject.

Key Stage 4

For Years 10 and 11, the requirements change somewhat.

As well as religious education (as an examination or non-examination subject) National Curriculum regulations require you to study:

Core	Foundation
Mathematics English Science* Welsh ‡	Technology A modern foreign language History† Geography† Physical education (not necessarily to GCSE) Welsh ‡

* Science

Science will be more usually offered as **balanced science** (an integration of physics, chemistry and biology). This can be studied as:

Single science 12.5% of the timetable

Double science 20% of the timetable

Double science will give you 2 GCSE awards.

The sciences can also be studied separately but if all 3 are taken, some 30% of the week will be used up.

† **History/geography**

The position of history and geography is special at Key Stage 4. The National Curriculum requires you to study EITHER

☞ full history, no geography OR

☞ full geography, no history OR

☞ 1/2 course of history + 1/2 course of geography OR a short course in both in relation to another area of the curriculum

Your school will offer some but not necessarily all these possibilities.

You will notice that no **Creative Subject** is compulsory but you are advised to consider its claims (see p 27).

‡In Wales, Welsh will be a core subject in schools where it is the language every subject is taught in; in the remaining schools, it will be a foundation subject.

Cross-Curricular Themes

Your school will also provide you with an education which meets the aims of the Education Reform Act with respect to preparing you for adult life and responsibilities. So, either directly linked to programmes of study and attainment targets or through personal and social education you will have to consider:

Careers education and guidance

Health education

Citizenship

Environmental education

Economic and industrial understanding

For an example of how these could apply, look at the chart which follows where each of them is related to a unit of work in **Modern foreign languages**. But remember, they apply to all subjects.

CROSS-CURRICULAR THEMES

Aspects of the five major cross-curricular themes are contained in the seven areas of experience. The table shows how a unit of MFL work might contribute to the themes, while reinforcing use of the target language.

AREA OF EXPERIENCE: Everyday activities
MFL THEME: Home life

CROSS-CURRICULAR THEME	POSSIBLE FOCUS IN THE TARGET LANGUAGE
ECONOMIC AND INDUSTRIAL UNDERSTANDING	▷ eating out ▷ family spending and household budgets ▷ personal spending, eg. pocket money ▷ advertising
HEALTH EDUCATION	▷ personal hygiene routines, eg. cleaning teeth ▷ exercise routines ▷ getting on with others ▷ safety in the home
CAREERS EDUCATION AND GUIDANCE	▷ typical working day of employees in other countries ▷ who does what in the home and why
ENVIRONMENTAL EDUCATION	▷ forms of travel and their effects on the environment ▷ sources of noise pollution, eg. stereos, washing machines ▷ products used in the home, eg. environmentally friendly products, fast foods
EDUCATION FOR CITIZENSHIP	▷ leisure activities ▷ rules at home, punishments and rewards

Is There Anything Left to Choose?

Most certainly – Yes! It was never the intention of the originators of the National Curriculum to fill the whole week. There remains a long list of possibilities for you to consider. These include:

> **Art**
> **Music**
> **Drama**
> **Classics (Latin or Greek)**
> **Sociology**
> **Home economics/food technology**
> **Economics**
> **Business studies**
> **Keyboard skills**
> **The history/geography alternatives**
> **The single/double science option**
> **Various forms of craft, design and technology.**

There is nothing to stop you 'doubling up' on preferred curriculum areas, ie taking two modern foreign languages, doubling business studies or CDT options.

A Word about Timing

Not all subjects listed above are yet compulsory for students starting Key Stage 4 in September 1993. Below is a timetable showing the present position. You should note however that many schools are organising their option studies now in anticipation of what is to come.

Timetable for introducing all the foundation subjects and reported assessment

| | | | Key Stage | | | |
			1	2	3	4
Mathematics and science	Introduction	Autumn	1989	1990	1989	1992
	First reported assessment	*Summer*	*1992*	*1995*	*1993*	*1994*
English	Introduction	Autumn	1989	1990	1990	1992
	First reported assessment	*Summer*	*1992*	*1995*	*1994*	*1994*
Technology	Introduction	Autumn	1990	1990	1990	1993
	First reported assessment	*Summer*	*1993*	*1995*	*1994*	*1995*
History and geography†	Introduction	Autumn	1991	1991	1991	1994
	First reported assessment	*Summer*	*1994*	*1996*	*1995*	*1996*
Art, music, PE and modern languages†	Introduction	Autumn	1992	1992	1992	1995
	First reported assessment	*Summer*	*1995*	*1997*	*1996*	*1997*
Welsh*	Introduction	Autumn	1990	1990	1990	1992
	First reported assessment	*Summer*	*1993*	*1995*	*1994*	*1994*

*This timetable applies to Welsh both as a core and as another foundation subject. Where Welsh is a foundation subject, the Working Group has proposed in its interim report that attainment targets and programmes of study be introduced for those schools which presently teach Welsh. For schools which do not currently teach the language, attainment targets and programmes of study should be introduced over a period of time but not later than September 1992.

† Provisional.

What if You are in an Independent (Private) School?

Private schools do not have to teach the National Curriculum but in reality many are already following it. They have appreciated the contribution it makes to breadth and balance and it makes more sense if all pupils have access to the same areas of learning experience. It also helps when students change schools and thereby move between the two systems.

5 Hurdles Ahead

This is the part you may think you won't like. First of all, however, cut exams down to size. They are not the most important part of the next two years. What you actually learn is far more valuable than any piece of paper which announces that you have a certificate in this or that. Certificates tell other people (employers or colleges) what subjects you have studied and the level you have reached in them. Think of exams as measuring instruments. You are not scared of scales or rulers, so you need not be frightened of exams if you have done your best over the past two years.

For some of you, public examinations will not be a new experience. Towards the end of Key Stage 3, many of you will have had your progress assessed by your teachers and you also will have taken Standard Attainment Tests (SATs) in mathematics, science and English. Taking your exams at the end of Key Stage 4 (at the end of Year 11) will just be an extension of this.

How Testing is Organised

In case you are not familiar with the new developments let's map out the whole testing procedure from the age of 6 to 16. Particularly as you are coming in part way through, you need to appreciate the whole picture.

1

Targets

What are you aiming for in your studies?

Every subject you learn will have attainment **targets**

Knowledge ie what you can remember

Understanding ie what you can explain

Skills ie what you can do

Levels

How well did you achieve those targets?

These targets can be achieved at a variety of **levels**

eg **Knowledge**	**Understanding**	**Skills**
A great deal	A thorough grasp	Very competent
↕	↕	↕
Secure in simple facts	Basic understanding	Can just cope

LEVELS
OF ACHIEVEMENT

The National Curriculum has 10 levels of achievement in each of the 10 curriculum subjects.

Children start working towards level 1 in each subject at the age of five. Different children will move up the levels at different speeds, but most are likely to move on by one level every two years.

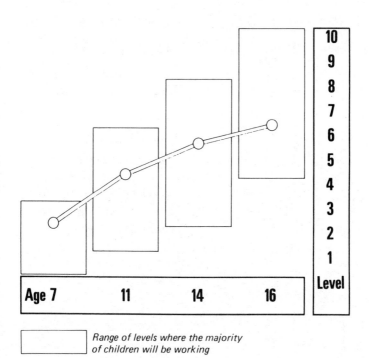

Range of levels where the majority of children will be working

The average level achieved

3 Milestones

When are these achievements measured?

Milestones along the way are now called **Key Stages**. Had your time in school so far been in the shadow of the National Curriculum, you would have passed through two stages before entering secondary school and you are now completing **Key Stage 3**.

You are assessed at the end of each Key Stage. The diagram below shows how your age relates to the milestones.

The levels you can achieve are numbered 1 to 10. The graph above shows how and when these levels could be secured— especially as you pass through **Key Stages 3** and **4**.

ASSESSMENT

Pupil progress is monitored continuously by teachers, but formal assessment takes place at the ages of 7, 11, 14 and 16. These ages mark the end of the four key stages which cover the 11 years of compulsory education.

AGES

Key Stage 1	5 – 7			
Key Stage 2		7 – 11		
Key Stage 3			11 – 14	
Key Stage 4				14 – 16

National Curriculum assessment is not a pass/fail system. It gives teachers the feedback they need to plan teaching at the right level for individual pupils; helps to identify learning difficulties; and provides information for parents and others.

The systematic record-keeping made possible by assessment helps to ensure progression, so that a different teacher or school can build on what the pupil has already achieved.

Reproduced by permission of the National Curriculum Council

How does all this relate to GCSE?

For those taking GCSE **at present**, there are 7 grades which are passes and an ungraded category which is a fail.

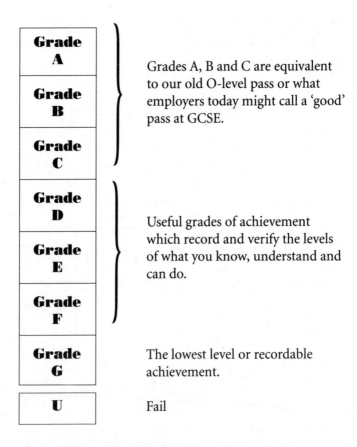

Grade A	
Grade B	Grades A, B and C are equivalent to our old O-level pass or what employers today might call a 'good' pass at GCSE.
Grade C	
Grade D	
Grade E	Useful grades of achievement which record and verify the levels of what you know, understand and can do.
Grade F	
Grade G	The lowest level or recordable achievement.
U	Fail

From 1994 it is **likely** that these grades will be progressively lined up with a National Curriculum extended scale of attainment targets from level 4 to level 10.

GCSE

Levels as measured in National Curriculum terms

GCSE	Levels	
Grade A	levels 9/10	
Grade B	level 8	
Grade C	level 7	all these assessed levels will be recorded on your GCSE certificates
Grade D		
Grade E	level 6	
Grade F	level 5	
Grade G	level 4	
U	ungraded equivalent to levels 1, 2 or 3	not recorded

There could also be an A+ category for any outstandingly good quality grade A achievements.

What Does This Mean for Your Timetabled Subjects?

All this means a much sharper focus for learning. What you are expected to know, understand and be good at can be **translated** into subject **theories** and **skills**. This should help you know where you are and where you are going – valuable pointers to help you eventually get there!

The attainment targets for

English

Mathematics

Science

Modern foreign languages

have been fully worked out for Key Stage 4.

SUBJECT ATTAINMENT TARGETS

Attainment targets define the knowledge, skills and understanding pupils are expected to have by the end of each key stage. Each of the attainment targets is defined further through statements of attainment spread over 10 levels of difficulty.

SUBJECT	ATTAINMENT TARGETS
ENGLISH	Speaking and listening; reading; writing; spelling; handwriting.
MATHEMATICS	Using and applying mathematics; number; algebra; shape and space; handling data.
SCIENCE	Scientific investigation; life and living processes; materials and their properties; physical processes.
TECHNOLOGY	Identifying needs and opportunities; generating a design; planning and making; evaluating; information technology capability.
HISTORY	Knowledge and understanding of history; interpretations of history; the use of historical sources.
GEOGRAPHY	Geographical skills; knowledge and understanding of places; physical geography; human geography; environmental geography.
MODERN FOREIGN LANGUAGES	Listening; speaking; reading; writing.
ART	Investigating and making; knowledge and understanding.
MUSIC	Performing and composing; listening and appraising.
PHYSICAL EDUCATION	End of key stage statements and programme of study (general), programmes of study (specific activity).

☞ Now let's take ☞

☞ a longer look at ☞

☞ GCSE ☞

☞ at present ☞

The General Certificate of Secondary Education

The important things about GCSE are:

☞ It is a single-subject exam. You can sit as few or as many subjects as you like. Those in which you achieve a grade will appear on your certificate.

☞ The normal age for sitting it will be 16+, at the end of Year 11. You can, however, take it earlier or later or more than once if your school advises it.

☞ GCSE is run by:

Six examining groups

The University of London Examinations and Assessment Council (ULEAC)
The Midland Examining Group (MEG)
The Northern Examining and Assessment Board (NEAB)
The Northern Ireland Schools Examination Council (NISEC)
The Southern Examining Group (SEG)
The Welsh Joint Education Committee (WJEC)

☞ Schools are free to choose their Groups, so you could sit exams run by different Groups. There will, however, be a common timetable operating over all.

☞ Certificates will be awarded on a single scale of seven grades.

☞ The exam is open to anyone.

Making Examinations Fair

How does anyone know that a grade C in English achieved in Berwick-on-Tweed is equivalent to a grade C in English taken in Bristol? What are the guarantees? How are they ensured? It would be unfair if one were easier than the other.

To ensure fairness and equality GCSE has certain safeguards which apply to the exam as a whole and to individual subjects. These safeguards will apply whichever Group's exams you sit. They are

National specifications for all exams

All the exams are designed to measure what you

Know
Understand
Can do

There will often be papers representing different levels of difficulty so that your knowledge, understanding and ability can be properly tested and you can be awarded a grade which fairly states just how good you are at a subject.

Guarantees Operating Within Subjects

These guarantees must be honoured by all the Examining Groups offering a particular subject. They require the Group to:

- ☛ Set out a clear title and make sure that the subject content does not overlap with any other.

- ☛ Explain clearly the aim of the course.

- ☛ Offer you enough experiences during the course to enable you to achieve any of the seven grades.

- ☛ Avoid making unreasonable demands on you.

- ☛ Try not to be too expensive.

- ☛ Provide opportunities both for your own teacher and an external examiner to have a say in your final result.

- ☛ Make the assessment objectives clear.

- ☛ Help you relate the course to life.

- ☛ Explain clearly exactly what can be expected from anyone who achieves them.

How You Will Be Awarded Your Grades

The seven GCSE grades cover an enormous range of talent – from the very good indeed to the reasonably competent. Examiners could measure this in a variety of ways.

For Example

1 Papers of increasing difficulty

The exam could be organised in a series of papers, or questions within papers, which get increasingly difficult.

or

There could be broad questions which everyone can answer but which have more demanding parts to them.

2 Common and optional papers

The exam could be organised in three papers. Everyone would take paper 2 after which candidates could choose between a more difficult paper 3 or an easier paper 1.

3 Grade-related papers

Under this system the papers you took would lead to a range of grades. For example:

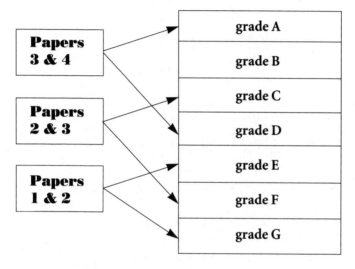

If you sat papers 1 & 2 only, your final result could only lie between grades E and G. It would not be possible to achieve a grade higher than E. To get higher grades you would have to take papers 2 and 3 which lead to a grade between C and F. In order to obtain a grade A you would have to take papers 3 and 4.

Your subject teacher will make clear to you how the GCSE papers you will sit are designed.

What About Coursework?

Everybody has heard about coursework! Rumours are rife and some people think they will be struck down by it like a disease, so let's get it into perspective. There are some basic points to be clear about.

☛ Every subject has some form of compulsory coursework.

☛ Coursework is important because it assesses what you can do outside a two-hour paper in an examination room – like managing a long-term investigation or playing in a musical group. It's all about what you can research on a topic and gives you an opportunity to show up well.

☛ It is important since at least 20% of the final result comes from the coursework mark. In many subjects it will be higher. See page 55.

☛ The principal difficulty is one of organisation and there will be some time-juggling to do. You may have several pieces of coursework on the go at the same time, being worked on partly at home and partly at school. If you feel snowed under, your first move is to talk it over with the appropriate subject teacher who will help you sort it out.

☛ Coursework does not suit the 'let's put it off until tomorrow' person. If you continually do this, you will not survive. Get down to it sensibly; think, plan and organise carefully and you will experience a great sense of achievement.

☛ Coursework can also be carried over into the sixth form and offered again in a retake of a GCSE exam.

☛ Spelling is now an important aspect which is tested in all subjects at GCSE. Five per cent of the marks are reserved for correct spelling in all subjects. This applies to both coursework and examination papers.

Coursework Limits* for Key Stage 4

Course beginning	Subject	Coursework limits
September 1992	English	40%†
	English Literature	30%
	Mathematics	20%
	Science	30%

† Up to 20% for Attainment Target 1 (Speaking and Listening) and up to 20% between Attainment Target 2 and 3 (Reading and Writing).

Course beginning	Subject	Coursework limits
September 1993	Biology	30%
	Chemistry	30%
	Physics	30%
	Technology	60%
September 1994	Geography	25%
	History	25%
September 1995	Modern Foreign Languages (provisional)	30%

* N.B. Some Examining Groups may set lower limits for coursework in particular syllabuses.

How Many Examination Subjects Should I Take?

It is difficult to generalise. Each person is different. If you are taking subjects which, at the time you are sitting the examination, are formally part of the National Curriculum foundation subjects, you will be required to have your abilities tested and examinations in these subjects will normally be compulsory.

As far as subjects outside the National Curriculum are concerned, take as many as you can without overstretching yourself. As you may not achieve all the grades you hope for, it is a good idea to take more subjects than you need, but don't go to extremes. It is better to obtain six GCSEs with good grades than ten GCSEs with low grades.

6 What Am I in For?

There is nothing like knowing where you are going! The broad journey plan suggesting a balance was set out on page 10, but you are now going to have to decide which subjects you will take in order to implement the plan. One way of choosing is to look at the aims of a course and the kind of examination that concludes it.

The national specifications and guidelines mentioned earlier set out exactly what a course is like and what the examiners are looking for.

In this chapter you will find:

☛ brief summaries of the course aims
☛ assessment objectives
☛ an indication of the form of the examination.

There is also another way to look at your future. You could use **Skills** as the starting point. On pages 90 and 91 you will see a table of skills which shows you the subjects in which they can be best developed.

Warning

In the pages which follow you must not assume that every aspect of the subject course and assessment objective is listed.

Here are only summaries, intended to convey a flavour of the programmes of study and assessment techniques ahead of you.

To find out more:

1.   List the subjects in which you are particularly interested
2.   Find out from your school which Examination Group's syllabus and exam is used
3.   Consult the full prospectus published by the Group
4.   Become familiar with the attainment targets published by the National Curriculum Council.

Art and design

The course is about expressing ideas with hand and eye and providing you with the opportunity of presenting your ideas, imagination and feelings creatively. If you choose this subject, your visual awareness should sharpen, your practical artistic skills develop, your self-confidence increase. You will be able to follow a broad course in art and design or specialise in one of the subject areas: drawing and painting; graphics; textiles; three-dimensional studies; photography.

In exploring elements like line, shape, form, colour, tone, pattern and texture, **you would be expected to:**

Know   Understand   Can do

☞ respond creatively to an idea, theme or subject

☞ record from direct observation or personal experience

☞ pursue a design from the idea stage to practical completion

☞ work on your own

☞ analyse ideas, research and communicate them

☞ blend materials, ideas and techniques sympathetically

☞ choose and use materials economically

☞ use and compose line, tone, colour, pattern, texture, shape, form and space.

Art is a subject which relies heavily on developing skills for success from Key Stage 1 to Key Stage 4. At all stages you should be making clear connections with artists who have made an important cultural contribution. The diagram below shows this for Key Stages 1 to 3 and you should expect this to continue throughout Key Stage 4.

The exam will include:

☞ **coursework:** either a selection of pieces, a special study or continuously assessed work

☞ **controlled test:** to show how well you can work on your own.

SUBJECT KNOWLEDGE: ART

Pupils need a developing grasp of 'what counts as art'. They need to look at, among other things:

O art from different cultures and times;

O pottery, weaving, clothing, buildings;

O posters, sculptures and paintings;

O television commercials;

O portraits;

O prints.

It is important that connections are made both to pupils' own work and to the connections between artists (AT 2, strand 2)

Pupils' practical work	Connections	Key Stage
Drawing and painting flowers	William Morris, van Gogh, Georgia O'Keefe	1
Experimenting with colours to represent 'sky'	Claude, Constable, Hiroshige	2
Using discarded objects to construct a new design	Picasso's use of a bicycle seat as the head of a bull; Miro	3
Experimenting with materials — clay, plaster, wire	Hepworth, Epstein, Giacometti, Cornell, Gabo, Schwitters	3
Painting trees in blossom	Palmer, Monet, the Indian and Persian miniaturists	2
Landscapes	Turner, Constable, Japanese wood blocks	3

Business studies

The aims of the **course** are that you should:

☞ know about the business world and how it works

☞ understand the way that major organisations affect business

☞ appreciate how competition and monopoly work

☞ explore the way in which commercial enterprises are organised, financed and work together

☞ understand the way that economics affect business activity

☞ find out how the business world affects society both in theory and from your own practical experience

☞ become aware of business language

☞ be able to select, handle and present information and data effectively

☞ become aware of the importance of change.

In the exam you will be expected to:

Know Understand Can do

☞ demonstrate your knowledge of the business world

☞ express ideas in words, figures and graphs

☞ show your understanding of business figures and themes

☞ choose, interpret and apply facts and figures

☞ solve business problems

☞ distinguish between evidence and opinion.

Know Understand Can do

The exam will comprise:
☞ written papers with particular emphasis on questions which present you with facts to work on
☞ possibly an oral examination
☞ compulsory coursework (which is likely to be about 25% of the total marks); it could be in the form of continuous assessment or a number of special assignments.

Classical subjects

This is an umbrella title which covers the Latin and Greek civilisations and the civilisations of their people's languages. It relates to language courses (indicated L below) and non-language courses (indicated NL below). The schemes are complex and interested students are strongly advised to consult the full syllabus.

The courses should enable you to:
☞ develop a competence in one of the languages (L)
☞ read, understand and appreciate some literature in the original (L) or in translation (NL), and respond to it (L and NL)
☞ understand the civilisation (L), paying particular attention to the art, literary and archaeological evidence (NL)
☞ appreciate the relationship of a classical language to English (L and NL)
☞ observe and analyse information critically (L and NL)

In the exam you will be expected to:

Language	Non-language
☞ demonstrate your language ability	☞ answer multiple-choice or stimulus questions to demonstrate your knowledge of the classical world
☞ show understanding of prepared texts in at least two of poetry, prose and drama	
☞ answer questions on literature, life, history and customs of Greece or Rome (between 10 and 25%).	☞ answer questions on literature in translation and show how evidence is used.

In the non-language course, assessed coursework will be required and will account for 20–25% of the marks.

Craft, Design and Technology*

The courses under this heading have one theme in common: your ability to exercise control over the made environment through a process which involves designing, making, testing and evaluating. Your school will probably offer a variety of courses which reflect this common aim but have different emphases:

☞ **CDT:** *design and realisation* – designing and making in wood, metal and plastics, with an emphasis on craft quality and good design.

☞ **CDT:** *technology* – designs which require the application of scientific and technical knowledge.

☞ **CDT:** *design and communication* – design with special attention to drawing and model-making.

* These courses are subject to revision in 1993.

The common aims of the three types of course are to:

Know | Understand | Can do

☞ describe and apply the principles/ideas of design to manufactured articles

☞ show which problems can be solved by practical or technological means

☞ enable you to design articles which look good and work

☞ evaluate finished products

☞ make sure good safety practices have been observed.

The exams of all the courses will test your:

☞ design skills

☞ making and assembling skills

☞ knowledge of principles

☞ ability to communicate.

The exams will include open-ended written questions and perhaps an oral test. You will be asked to solve design problems and to make articles. Your personal folio of work which could include mock-ups or models, will be important.

Coursework could account for up to 60% of your marks.

Economics

The aim of the course is to help you to understand how the world's scarce resources might best be used. You will learn how the British economy works and how it affects individuals, groups and organisations. You will pick up the language and terms economists use and get some practice in handling facts and figures. The ability to distinguish between evidence and opinion will be important. At the end of the course you should be in a better position to make informed decisions both as a consumer and a producer.

In the exam you will be expected to:

☞ recall and understand the principal facts which lie behind the way the economy works

☞ use this knowledge in words, calculations, graphs and pictures

☞ show you can use the appropriate terms properly

☞ choose, analyse, interpret and apply facts and figures

☞ distinguish between evidence and opinion, making sensible judgments and expressing them.

Know Understand Can do

The exam will consist of:

☞ **question papers** containing a variety of approaches – short answers, multiple choice, structured essays or continuous writing

☞ **coursework** assessed by your teachers, carrying 25% of the marks.

Science

The aims of the course set out below are consistent with the requirements of the National Curriculum Order for science and describe the educational purposes of a National Curriculum course for the GCSE examination in Science: Double Award or Science: Single Award.

1 To provide, through the exploration and study of science, a coherent educational experience which enables you to acquire sufficient understanding and knowledge to:

☞ become confident citizens in a technological world, able to take or develop an informed interest in matters of scientific import

☞ recognise the usefulness, and limitations of scientific methods and appreciate their applicability in other disciplines and in everyday life

☞ be encouraged to pursue and be suitably prepared for further studies in science.

2 To develop abilities and skills that:

☞ are relevant to the study, practice and application of science

☞ are useful in everyday life

☞ encourage safe practice.

3 To stimulate:

☞ curiosity, interest and enjoyment in science and its methods of enquiry

☞ interest in, and care for, the environment.

4 To promote awareness that:

☞ the study and practice of science are co-operative and cumulative activities and are subject to social, economic, technological, ethical and cultural influences and limitations

☞ the application of science may be both beneficial and detrimental to the individual, the community and the environment

☞ the concepts of science are of a developing and sometimes temporary nature.

Different examining groups will arrange their programmes of study in different ways. Below is an example from the Midland Examination Group.

Syllabus

This syllabus covers 18 topics to be studied over 2 years.

---

1 Sound & Hearing	11 Energy Flow & Ecosystems
2 Light & Sight	12 Weather & Atmosphere
3 Space & Communication	13 Rocks
4 Feedback & Control	14 Plants
5 Raw Materials	15 Animals
6 Reactions	16 The Body at Work
7 Structures & Properties	17 Plants at Work
8 Patterns & Trends	18 Forces & Machines
9 Electricity & Magnetism	
10 Fuels & Energy Sources	

Assessment objectives

For a full statement, you should consult the National

Curriculum statement of attainment targets, but in summary, they highlight

☞ **Scientific investigation** – how good you are at:
- asking questions, making predictions and developing theories
- observing, measuring, and handling variable factors
- interpreting results and evaluating scientific evidence.

☞ **Knowing and understanding science**
- an appreciation of life and living processes
- a knowledge and understanding of materials and their properties as well as physical processes
- the ability to communicate scientific observations, select data, interpret it and make deductions
- the ability to use science to solve problems.

(margin labels: Know   Understand   Can do)

The EXAM is designed to cater for different levels of ability and you will find that different papers lead to different National Curriculum attainment levels.

Tier	Levels Description	available	Duration
1	Written paper 1	3 to 6	1hr 15min
	Written paper 2	3 to 6	1hr 15min
2	Written paper 3	5 to 8	1hr 45min
	Written paper 4	5 to 8	1hr 45min
3	Written paper 5	7 to 10	2hr
	Written paper 6	7 to 10	2hr

Example from the Midland Examining Group

75% of the GCSE is provided from written examination
and 25% from internal assessment by teachers
(coursework).

You will be entered for the tier (1, 2 or 3) most
appropriate to your progress.

Other science issues

Names – You may find science referred to as Balanced,
Integrated, Modular or Separate. Each has a different
emphasis:

☞ **Balanced** – where separate areas are clear but all 3
science strands are studied in conjunction with each
other

☞ **Integrated** – where theories are arranged to stress
inter-relationships and particular ideas

☞ **Modular** –where theories are organised into separate
units of teaching and assessment

☞ **Separate** – where physics, chemistry and biology are
taught independently of each other.

Single or double?

This will be a matter of personal preference but you
should be aware of certain careers limitations if only
single balanced science is chosen (see page 116).

Science is not in a vacuum

You should never see any of your subjects in isolation one
from another. Science is a good example where

☞ important connections are made across the
curriculum with other **Subjects**

☞ **Skills** are developed which, of themselves, are not
only related to science

☞ **Themes** are involved which go well beyond the
subject areas which science normally covers

☞ **Dimensions** are explored which are common to every
subject.

To make this clear, look at the spidery network set out
overleaf.

SCIENCE LINKS

English

Know Understand Can do

The aims of the English course

are that you should:

☞ understand facts, ideas and opinions as you pass on information

☞ be critical of what you read and be able to sort out ideas for particular purposes

☞ be able to talk about experiences

☞ know how the English language is structured

☞ be able to use spoken English

☞ be aware of the differences between formal and informal English.

There are 3 attainment targets.

They are:

☞ **Speaking and listening,** in which you will have the chance to show how well you can:

☞ put experience into words, expressing what you feel and imagine

☞ understand, order and present facts, ideas and opinions

☞ show a sense of audience and an awareness of style in a variety of situations

☞ recognise different levels and kinds of meaning in a variety of contexts

☞ make a personal response to what you hear, read and understand

☞ reflect on the way other people communicate.

Know Understand Can do

☞ **Reading**, in which you will be able to show that you can:
☞ get hold of facts, ideas and opinions
☞ recognise different sorts of meanings
☞ understand how writers use language to get the effects they want.
☞ **Writing.** You will have plenty of opportunity to show you can:
☞ write about personal feelings
☞ understand and present facts, ideas and opinions
☞ show you can appreciate good grammar by using it well
☞ understand how flexible a tool language is to express what you want to say.

Correct spelling, good handwriting and careful presentation will all be important here!

Coursework could count for up to 40% of the marks (see above page 55).

Your assessment

There will be coursework and a final examination which can be sat in 3 tiers (or expected levels of outcome). You can only sit for one tier. They are arranged in this kind of pattern. Details will, however, vary between examination groups.

Level awarded

(Target levels ringed)

Tier 1   (4) (5)   6

Tier 2   5   (6) (7) (8) (9)   10

Tier 3   7   (8) (9) (10)

Example from WJEC

English literature

This is a separate examination but it follows the same pattern as English Language. In particular **you would be expected to:**

Know Understand Can do

☞ get to know the literature well

☞ understand the themes beneath the surface

☞ recognise the ways that writers achieve their effects

☞ understand the way human characteristics are portrayed

☞ make a personal and informed response to the literature being studied.

Results

For both examinations the results of GCSE in English will appear in National Curriculum terms as follows:

GCSE Grade	NC Level
A	10
	9
B	8
C	7
D	
E	6
F	5
G	4
U	

Drama

Your school may offer drama (sometimes called theatre studies) as one of its Creative Arts options. It is an important and exciting option but you need to be clear about its intentions. The course is NOT there to produce actors or stage technicians.

In the world of work employers are seeking people with well-developed personal qualities,
☞ people who can solve problems
☞ people who can think on their feet
☞ people who are totally reliable
☞ people who can work in teams
☞ people who can communicate well.

Drama provides all these skills. All theatre productions you have ever seen are good only if those skills are highly developed on and behind the stage. In addition, success in a subject like this can give you plenty of personal satisfaction and a lifelong leisure interest.

In the course you would be working on prepared pieces – performances based on a variety of texts as well as self-devised pieces, where, as a team you would be writing and acting a script for a specific audience – like producing a play on the theme of 'change' for junior schools. You would be learning about acting, design and technical support; be introduced to improvisation and scriptwriting as well as studying text interpretation. Opportunities are likely to be taken to visit theatres frequently.

Know | Understand | Can do

For the exam, the assessment is a practical business and you would be tested on your ability to:

☞ understand how a piece of drama is devised
☞ demonstrate technique
☞ organise a performance
☞ interpret a script
☞ be aware of the contribution of design and technology
☞ appreciate performances of others
☞ explore social and personal issues through the medium of drama.

Geography

The aim of the geography COURSE is to give you an understanding of the nature of the Earth's surface, the character of places and how human beings interact with their environment. Your studies will include enquiries on small, regional, national and international scales. Overall the course should enable you to make more sense of the world and encourage you to hold informed views on rapidly changing world issues.

Know | Understand | Can do

In the exam you will be expected to:

☞ show an awareness of places in relation to others
☞ explain your understanding of environments and the processes which affect them (economic and technological developments)

Know	Understand	Can do	
			☞ show that you understand how people interact with their environment
			☞ be aware of communities and cultures both in our society and elsewhere
			☞ demonstrate a range of skills developed through practical work: observing, fact-finding and analysis, using books, maps and photographs
			☞ show sensitivity to the environment and awareness of the contrasts between rich and poor nations.

The exam will include one or more question papers containing a variety of stimulus questions – maps, photographs and statistics to analyse and comment on. Your fieldwork, coursework and regular assignments will be assessed by your teachers, and will count for at least 20% (but not more than 25%) of the overall final mark.

History

The history course will bring the past alive. It will encourage you to develop an enthusiasm for using the evidence to discover what it was like to live in a different time from your own, and to make comparisons. Whatever period of history you study, you will explore cause and consequence, continuity and change, similarity and difference. The development of particular skills will be important: how to find out information from first-hand

sources and from other people's writings, how to spot
bias, how to present what you have discovered in a logical
way. Hopefully you will develop an interest in history
which will continue long after you leave school.

Know Understand Can do

In the exam you will be expected to:
☞ recall and select knowledge, setting it out
clearly
☞ show that you understand something of the
pattern of historical development
☞ prove you can explore history using a variety
of sources – evidence of the time, objects,
books, statistics and word of mouth
☞ interpret your findings, sorting out fact from
opinion and detecting bias
☞ reach balanced conclusions.

The exam will include:
☞ **questions** which will ask you to respond to a
variety of forms of historical evidence
☞ **short-answer questions** to test knowledge
and understanding
☞ **questions** which require you to write
continuous prose, but not necessarily long
essays
☞ **coursework** assessed by your teachers,
accounting for at least 20% of your marks
(but not more that 25%).

Home Economics

The course in home economics explores the physical,
social, economic and design needs of the home in general,
and food, clothing and shelter in particular. It helps you,
as a future homemaker, to improve your skills in
managing resources and helps you to become an effective
member of a family, of the community and of society.
Both theory and practice are seen as important and there
will be emphasis on problem-solving and decision-

making. Home economics covers the home, family, food and textiles and the application of human skill, effort, money, time and materials to them. You will be expected to investigate, analyse, interpret and discriminate before turning theory into practice. After covering this common background, you will be able to specialise in one aspect of the home: family, food or textiles.

Know Understand Can do

In the exam you will be expected to:
☞ appreciate how aspects of homemaking work together
☞ explain human needs at various stages of life
☞ know how a family works as an effective unit
☞ prove you have the skills to meet short-term needs and to appreciate long-term needs
☞ be aware of technological changes and how they affect the home
☞ display a critical awareness of advertising
☞ know the requirements of good safety practices.
The exam will include: a variety of written and practical tests.

Mathematics

The mathematics course aims to increase your confidence by improving your skills in oral, written and practical maths. It endeavours to give you a feel for numbers and to enable you to understand the meaning of the results you get. Problem-solving, presentation and result-checking are important as is coming to grips with mathematical principles. The broader aspects of maths will not be ignored – applying maths to everyday situations and understanding the part it plays in the world around you. You will be expected to recognise when new situations can best be represented mathematically and to decide which methods are best suited to solve problems. The relationship between maths and science and technology will be made clear, as will the patterns and relationships within the subject itself. Individual enquiry and experiment will be important as you develop the ability to reason logically, classify, generalise and prove. Essentially, maths is communication.

In the exam you will be expected to:

Know | Understand | Can do

☞ recall, use and apply maths in many situations using your problem-solving skills clearly and logically

☞ use tables, graphs and diagrams

☞ understand measurement using appropriate instruments (including calculators) accurately

Know Understand Can do	

☞ recognise and express patterns in maths

☞ carry out practical work on an extended basis.

The exam will not include a common paper to suit all grades. You will take an end-of-course paper appropriate to your ability.

☞ **Coursework** will account for 20% of the marks.

Attainment targets

There are 5 of these, each one containing 3 or 4 strands.

Attainment targets	Strands
1 Using and applying mathematics	Applications Mathematical communication Reasoning, logic and proof
2 Number	Knowledge and use of numbers Estimation and approximation Measures
3 Algebra	Patterns and relationships Formulae, equations and inequalities Graphical representation
4 Shape and space	Shape Location Movement Measures
5 Handling data	Collecting and processing Representing and interpreting Probability

Levels of assessment

The exams themselves are arranged on a three-tier basis, very similar to the pattern for English and science. An example from the Southern Examining Group:

Levels awarded (Target levels ringed)

Foundations	③	④	⑤	⑥	7		
Intermediate		4	⑤	⑥	⑦	⑧	9
Higher			6	⑦	⑧	⑨	⑩

Great care should be taken in selecting the level of examination taken. A weak candidate choosing the higher level papers, just failing to achieve level 7 would not get a 6, but an ungraded result.

Modern Foreign Languages

You have only to spend a holiday outside the United Kingdom in continental Europe to be aware of the importance of a modern foreign language. You can't go far without some skill in it, if you are going to appreciate what is going on around you and make yourself understood.

But it's not just a matter of speaking to understand and be understood. A study of MFL (as they are increasingly called) will introduce you to the culture and civilisation of the country and help you appreciate it better. Using the target language chosen is intended to be both enjoyable and intellectually stimulating not just between you and your teacher in school but beyond the classroom to the world outside for the rest of your life.

Your confidence and experience is built up through many sorts of contacts you make each time you have an MFL lesson.

USING THE TARGET LANGUAGE

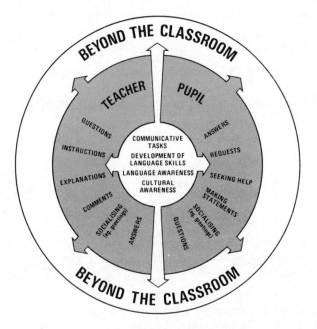

BEYOND THE CLASSROOM

TEACHER PUPIL

QUESTIONS

INSTRUCTIONS

EXPLANATIONS

COMMENTS

SOCIALISING (eg. greetings)

ANSWERS

COMMUNICATIVE TASKS
DEVELOPMENT OF LANGUAGE SKILLS
LANGUAGE AWARENESS
CULTURAL AWARENESS

ANSWERS

REQUESTS

SEEKING HELP

MAKING STATEMENTS

SOCIALISING (eg. greetings)

QUESTIONS

BEYOND THE CLASSROOM

Reproduced by permission of the National Curriculum Council

Because it is so important MFL will be gradually phased in as a compulsory part of the National Curriculum. These are the expected milestone dates.

Programme for modern foreign languages in the National Curriculum

November 1991	Parliament agreed
Spring 1992	NCC published modern foreign language guidance for schools
August 1992	National Curriculum modern foreign language introduced in Key Stage 3
Summer 1995	The first Key Stage 3 assessments will be held
August 1995	National Curriculum modern foreign language will be introduced at Key Stage 4
Summer 1997	First National Curriculum assessment at Key Stage 4 will be held

© NCC January 1992

Know Understand Can do

In the years prior to these developments at Key Stage 4, you will be **expected to show some ability** in

☞ **Listening** – understanding announcements, requests and conversations

☞ **Reading** – understanding public notices and signs like menus, timetables and brochures

☞ **Speaking** – responding to unprepared questions using language sounds which a sympathetic native speaker could understand

☞ **Writing**

☞ **Coursework** could account for up to 40% of your marks.

In the future it is likely that learning a modern foreign language at Key Stages 3 and 4 will look like this.

PROGRAMMES OF STUDY AND ATTAINMENT TARGETS

PROGRAMMES OF STUDY PART I:
LEARNING AND USING THE TARGET LANGUAGE

1   Communicating in the target language
2   Understanding and responding
3   Developing language learning skills and awareness of language
4   Developing cultural awareness
5   Developing the ability to work with others
6   Developing the ability to learn independently

PROGRAMMES OF STUDY PART II:
AREAS OF EXPERIENCE

Pupils must explore seven areas of experience over the period of each Key Stage. The areas of experience are:

Area A: Everyday Activities
Area B: Personal and Social Life
Area C: The World Around Us
Area D: The World of Education, Training and Work
Area E: The World of Communications
Area F: The International World
Area G: The World of Imagination and Creativity

ATTAINMENT TARGETS

AT1   Listening ● The development of pupils' ability to understand and respond to spoken language

AT2   Speaking ● The development of pupils' ability to communicate in speech

AT3   Reading ● The development of pupils' ability to read, understand and respond to written language

AT4   Writing ● The development of pupils' ability to communicate in writing

---

Reproduced by permission of the National Curriculum Council

Each of the areas of study will develop a pattern of its own but to show the kind of achievements which studying an MFL can generate, look at these possibilities.

AREA G:
THE WORLD OF IMAGINATION
AND CREATIVITY

The interest and motivation of young learners can be stimulated by themes which relate to play and leisure — themes of fantasy, fiction and fun. **Area G** — the World of Imagination and Creativity — is an area of experience in its own right, and also pervades the other AoE.

Activities might include:

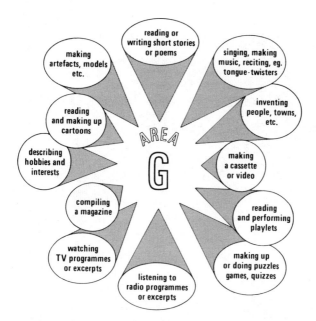

reading or writing short stories or poems

singing, making music, reciting, eg. tongue-twisters

making artefacts, models etc.

inventing people, towns, etc.

reading and making up cartoons

making a cassette or video

describing hobbies and interests

AREA G

compiling a magazine

reading and performing playlets

watching TV programmes or excerpts

making up or doing puzzles games, quizzes

listening to radio programmes or excerpts

Earlier in this section we said that you should not regard science as a subject in a vacuum. The same is true of your modern foreign languages. A similar (but not the same) spidery network links it in with so many other areas and activities within and beyond the school.

LINKS

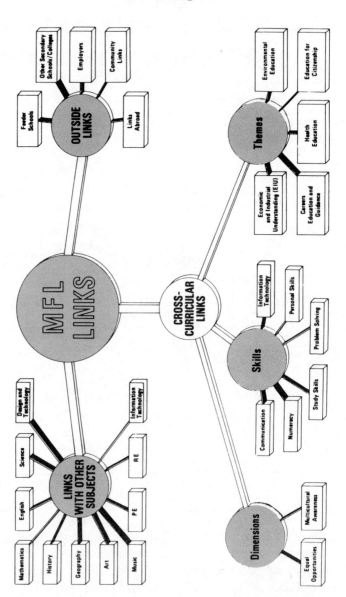

Reproduced by permission of the National Curriculum Council

Music

The course in music is essentially a practical one. Its aim is to provide you with extended musical experience which will improve your skills and stimulate your imagination. The course includes listening, performing and composing and will feature music of all kinds. You will be encouraged to get behind the music to the thoughts and feelings of the composer, and you will be introduced to the skills of analysis and co-ordination which should increase your enjoyment of music.

Know Understand Can do

In the exam you will be expected to:
☞ listen and respond to music, using technical and non-technical language to show you are aware of musical style and construction
☞ perform – you will be required to offer two of the following: singing or playing individually or in a group, or rehearsing and directing a group; some unprepared performance will be required
☞ compose – you will try your hand at composing during the course and this will count towards your final grade.

The exam will be essentially practical with written papers to assess the listening part of the course. You will be assessed on genuine musical activities in the life of the school rather than on examination test pieces. You should note, however, that holding a grade from another music examination board will not exempt you from any part of the GCSE.

Increasingly you will find opportunities to develop skills through a number of subjects. Take information technology for example – it has more application to Key Stage 4 Music than you might at first think.

EXAMPLES OF DEVELOPING INFORMATION TECHNOLOGY CAPABILITY IN MUSIC

Communicating information	○ using synthesizers, keyboards, computers, tape recorders, microphones to enable pupils to develop, organise and perform sounds ○ translation of sound into notations – printing notation
Handling information	○ data storage of sounds – a sound bank ○ CD ROM – interactive programmes developing historical knowledge ○ multi-tracking – recording and mixing
Modelling	○ using preset forms – composing within a defined musical structure
Measurement and control	○ mixing desks ○ 'expression' pedals/controllers ○ synthesis of sounds ○ using MIDI ○ sound sampling
Evaluating applications	○ analysis of modern music which uses electronic means to compose and improvise ○ comparing live and recorded performances

Reproduced by permission of the National Curriculum Council

Not yet part of the National Curriculum at Key Stage 4, but still important to the balance of your academic studies; do not underestimate the importance of

Physical education

in its many and various forms. Some schools may offer it to GCSE level.

AREAS OF ACTIVITY

Athletics activities

Dance

Games

Gymnastic activities

Outdoor and adventurous activities

Swimming

A summary of some GCSE subjects and the main personal skills you need to be successful in them Note that the absence of an $*$ in a grid does not mean that the particular skill will never be required **Principal skills being examined**	Art and design	Craft/Design/Technology	Drama
1 Calculating		*	
2 Communicating	*	*	*
3 Distinguishing between fact and opinion			
4 Interpreting creatively	*	*	*
5 Observing	*	*	*
6 Solving problems	*	*	*
7 Selecting materials	*	*	
8 Setting up experiments		*	
9 Showing an interest in the environment	*	*	*
10 Showing an interest in living things			
11 Using a language other than English			
12 Working independently	*	*	*
13 Recalling		*	*
14 Understanding yourself and others			*

ome subjects offered at GCSE

Classical subjects	Computer studies	Economics	English	Modern foreign languages	Geography	History	Home economics	Mathematics	Music	Religious studies	Science (in combination)	Social science
	*	*			*	*	*	*			*	*
*	*	*	*	*	*	*	*	*	*	*	*	*
*		*	*		*	*	*			*	*	*
			*			*	*		*			*
*			*	*	*	*	*	*	*		*	*
	*				*	*	*	*			*	*
						*	*				*	*
	*					*	*	*			*	*
*		*		*	*	*				*	*	*
				*						*	*	
*	*			*				*	*			
*	*	*	*	*	*	*	*	*	*	*	*	*
*	*	*	*	*	*	*	*	*	*	*	*	*
*			*	*	*	*	*			*		*

Religious studies

The religious studies course is open to people of all religions and to those with no religious faith at all. It is a course based on understanding rather than commitment. It will enquire into individual and group expressions of belief, trying to find out what religion is all about and show how it is reflected in what people experience, believe and do. Important life-centred questions will be asked especially in relation to the traditional attitudes and practices of various faiths. Some syllabuses will concentrate on one religion while others will take a wider view. Moral questions will not be ignored and the achievement of religion in shaping human beliefs and behaviour will be considered.

Know **Understand** **Can do**	**In the exam** you will be expected to: ☞ show an understanding of language, terms and ideas used in religion ☞ appreciate special people, writings and traditions in religion ☞ be clear about the main beliefs of the religion studied ☞ understand the pros and cons of issues ☞ attempt questions about the meaning of life and the variety of responses which religion gives to such questions

Know	Understand	Can do

☞ show you understand the difference between evidence, argument and faith.

In no way will the exam test your personal faith.

☞ **Coursework**, assessed by your teacher, will account for 20-30% of the marks.

☞ There will be a variety of written questions from short-answer questions to extended essays, but you should note that you will be allowed to take copies of set texts into the exam, so your memory will not have to do overtime.

Social science

The social science course looks at groups of people and explores how they live, work and relate to one another.

You will study aspects of society, its economy and politics. The point of such a course is to give you a wide background against which to set your everyday experiences. Moral values also find a place in the course and you will learn to use evidence to support judgments. You will study other cultures and the course will also enable you to appreciate how society has changed. You will be trained and will gain experience in handling data.

Know Understand Can do

In the exam you will be expected to:

☞ show that you understand what today's society is like and how it has come to its present form

☞ apply that knowledge to your everyday life and changes that may occur in the future

☞ take a considered look at social, economic and political arrangements

☞ know how to use scientific method to collect facts, analyse them and draw conclusions

☞ use language, figures and graphs to come to points of view

☞ distinguish between evidence and opinion.

The exam is likely to be based on written papers which include:

☞ material (such as photographs and newspaper cuttings) to set you thinking

☞ questions involving the use of words and figures

☞ short-answer questions and free-response essays

☞ **Compulsory coursework** will account for at least 20% of the final mark.

7 Where Does it Lead?

It all looks so obvious. All you have to do is choose your career and fit your subjects to it. The way is marked out from before 14 through to 18, or is it?

If it were all as easy as this, there would be no need to write a book about it.

The snag is that at 14 years old, when you are doing the choosing, you may not have a clue about your future career. Only one thing is certain: by the time you are 16 you will probably be a different person – your career ideas may well have changed. The world will not have stood still either. There may be opportunities opening up which you had not dreamed of and there will be others you were relying on which may be disappearing.

Here is a list of careers you would not have considered had you left school in 1960, since they were either just beginning to appear or had not been invented.

New careers since the 1960s	
teacher or administrator in the Open University customs and excise officer working on VAT audio engineer in stereo sound hypermarket manager computer programmer colour television engineer traffic warden micro-electronics engineer	oil-rig engineer in the UK sports or recreation centre administrator genetic counsellor aeronautical engineer in supersonic aviation credit-card administrator systems analyst consumer protection officer

Many careers that might once have seemed futuristic are emerging, but openings in them are still reasonably scarce.

robot calibrators
Third World agro-economist
home computer terminal engineers
alternative technology scientists
heliport terminal staff
artificial food producers
weather controllers
data system specialists
highway automative controllers

How then do we cope with the unknown? How do you choose from a fixed list of subjects when your own personality and the job world are both changing? Fortunately there are certain fixed points.

1 Make sure your subject choice leaves you flexible.
2 Try to keep career doors open for as long as possible.
3 If you have a broad idea of a career make sure you cover subject requirements.
4 Be prepared to retrain and learn new skills some time in the future.

There are some subject areas which you should consider very carefully because they have a bearing now on career openings.

English

If you are aiming at a career which demands high communication skills, English at a good grade level will be a top priority. Sometimes English literature is an acceptable alternative.

History

This is not a subject which is compulsory for any career but you should note that it is sometimes an acceptable alternative for courses which require a subject testing your command of English.

Maths

A very important subject, almost as widely demanded as English. There are, however, some careers which do not demand a GCSE maths qualification of grade C or above.

Modern Foreign and Classical Languages

A knowledge of German can be very useful to the scientist – many technical papers are written in the language. You no longer have to have a classical subject to GCSE level before you can go to university. Now that

Britain is a member of the EC, languages are even more important for all kinds of careers.

Computer Studies

As computers are rapidly becoming everyday tools in a wide range of careers, it is important to be reasonably proficient in keyboard skills. It is *not* however, a necessity to take GCSE computer studies which is largely a subject for those interested in computing for its own sake.

Science

Until recently science options were usually a three-way affair – a choice between the claims of physics, chemistry or biology (or perhaps a combination of two of them). There have been problems in this arrangement – not least the high proportion who drop physics and the undue attention given to biology by girls. This is hardly an appropriate situation for a technological society.

Balanced science may be offered in your school as a mean of integrating the three elements, mixing practical skills, processes and content extracted from each of the previous scientific areas. In this way, by avoiding repetition and choosing the most relevant areas from each, it is hoped that your scientific education will be better planned and close no door in the future. It would probably take 20% of the timetable and could lead to double certification in science.

Such integrated courses dovetail into A-level and are acceptable to universities seeking a broad, balanced education, though for some science degrees, the possession of AS-level in the science you are not taking as A-level could be important. For those not intending to proceed to higher education it is an excellent broadly based foundation.

Specialist areas

There are several specialist areas. Any pupil who intends to go in for one of the specialist subjects, like the creative arts, would be well advised to include the appropriate subjects at this stage.

Business subjects

Economics is a valuable subject to understand how the present day business world works. Some schools offer a course which includes shorthand, typing, accounts and office practice. Others offer separate subjects which you can add to your choice.

Clearly these are important for anyone who wishes to work in an office. From a career point of view, however, you need to distinguish between the business specialism and the commercial support services. A banker is a specialist, the secretary who works in a bank provides a support service. Secretarial skills are useful, but if you are aiming to work in business as a specialist it is better to have a broad range of GCSEs than to concentrate on office skills. If you are aiming to join the support services as a typist, receptionist or clerical assistant for example, office skills are invaluable and provide a useful foundation on which to build.

Technology

A wide range of creative subjects appears under the technical studies umbrella: areas of applied technology, design studies, design and realisation, engineering workshop theory and practice, electronics, plastics, engineering and materials science. In the new exam they have been brought together under more easily recognisable names. Many of these newer courses are based on problem-solving and include project work. They provide excellent experience for everyone, not just those considering engineering as a career. These courses are also useful for those who wish to acquire the technological literacy essential to understanding the modern world.

Are Some Subjects More 'Valuable' Than Others?

Teachers will say 'no'. Some employers will say 'yes'. Since they look at the question from different viewpoints it is possible for both to be right.

Teachers' point of view

Many teachers will say that all school subjects are part of human knowledge. To be good at one therefore is equal to being good in another. A GCSE grade C in physics is neither better nor worse than a GCSE grade C in music. The areas of study are different and cannot be compared.

Employers' point of view

Some employers and professional bodies look at GCSEs in the light of the skills they need in their businesses. For example, the personnel manager in an engineering firm may say that a GCSE grade C in science is essential and refuse to take a grade C in art into consideration. On the other hand, a higher education admissions tutor selecting potential primary-school teachers might well say that a GCSE grade C in art is just as important as one in science.

To obtain more insight into why some employers look with special interest at some subjects more than others, try the exercise following the chart below.

Each horizontal line must add up to 20	English	Maths	Science	Modern Foreign Language	Humanity (eg history, geography)	Creative subject (eg art)	
Airline cabin crew							20
Barrister							20
Bus conductor							20
Doctor							20
Hairdresser							20
Museum curator							20
Plumber							20
Research physicist							20
Secretary							20
Telephone operator							20

Talking points

1 Imagine you are an employer in each of the ten careers listed on page 103.
2 Taking one career at a time, consider the principal school subjects listed along the top.
3 Give yourself 20 points per line. Divide them up according to how important you think the subject is to the career.
4 Compare answers with a friend. Do you disagree? Why?
5 How valuable would each of the subjects in the chart be if you chose the careers listed?

What If Exams Are Not For Me?

You would not be the first to think that way. Some people can do them. Some can't.

To be unable to perform well in exams is not the end of the world. There are several points which should cheer you up if you are not a champion exam-passer.

☞ The course you follow is more important than the exam you sit at the end of it.

☞ Putting a lot of effort into subjects can be just as rewarding as getting graded at the end of the course.

☞ There are still career areas where interesting jobs need experience of certain subjects and good references rather than exam qualifications.

JOBS for which exams are **not** essential

Clerical

Typing, telephony, clerical and reception work. These and similar jobs are done in offices and can involve dealing with people and using simple office machinery. Your setting could be anywhere from a travel agency to a bank – big or small.

Useful School Subjects
English, maths, geography, social studies.

Creative

Creative jobs include music, dancing, drama, floristry, modelling and dressmaking. These jobs need flair, skill and lots of luck. In some of them you have to pass exams to obtain more responsible jobs. So you could have to face exams later on.

Useful School Subjects:
English and the subject which most reflects your skills.

JOBS for which exams are **not** essential

Practical

This is the biggest group and the jobs call for skills which cannot be tested in exams. Sewing machining, plastering, driving (over 18), painting and decorating, plumbing, packing, cookery and fire fighting (over 18) and many others, depending on where you live.

Useful School Subjects: CDT, English, Home economics, Food technology, mathematics.

Social

Social jobs involve meeting people and helping people. If you like doing this you could become a hairdresser, canteen assistant, shop assistant, hotel receptionist, mother's help, residential care assistant.

Useful School Subjects: English, history, social studies.

JOBS for which exams are **not** essential

Practical/ Scientific

Farm work, gardening, cookery, machine operating and work as a care assistant are all jobs needing a background of interest in one sort of science.

Useful School Subjects: Single science.

Outdoor

Farm, stable and kennel work, gardening, for example, are all done out of doors. These jobs are easier to find in the country than in the town, so you may have to travel.

Useful School Subjects: Single science, English, maths.

8 What Shall I Need?

It is one thing to know which subjects have a bearing on a particular career and quite another to act on that knowledge. 'What shall I need?' is a question you can answer only after taking all the relevant facts into consideration. A good starting point is your career plan as it stands now, however sketchy it may be.

On the next page there are other points to check.

The simple message is that all subjects of the curriculum are important. When they are assessed together at the end of Key Stage 4 and the results announced, it is like looking at the quality of a single diamond with a collection of polished faces. No face is more important than any other, but if any one is of poor quality, it will reduce the value of the whole jewel.

We have to be realistic however. Few people are good at everything and if some grades are poor, there will be career implications. It is not easy to be precise but the lists below will give you some ideas of doors which may close on you following the announcement of GCSE results.

Check your course ahead against your career plans

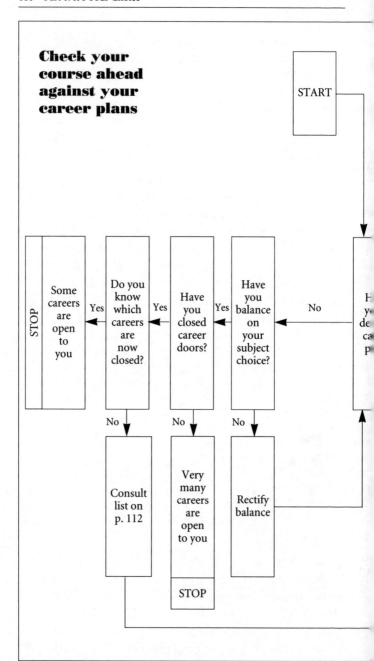

START

Have you decided career plans?

No →

Have you balance on your subject choice?

Yes →

Have you closed career doors?

Yes →

Do you know which careers are now closed?

Yes →

Some careers are open to you

STOP

No ↓ (Have you balance) → Rectify balance

No ↓ (closed career doors) → Very many careers are open to you — STOP

No ↓ (know which careers) → Consult list on p. 112

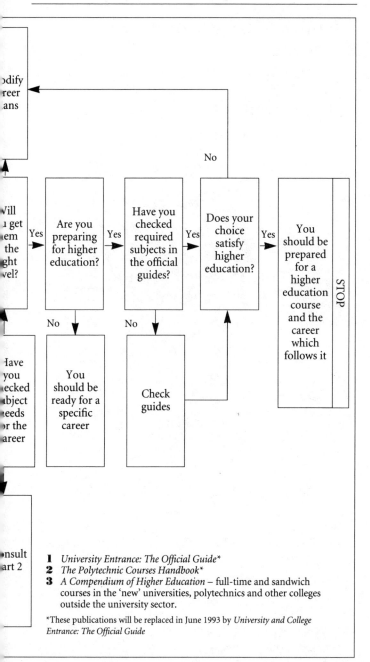

odify
reer
ans

Will
u get
em
the
ght
vel?

Yes → Are you preparing for higher education?

No

→ Have you checked required subjects in the official guides?

Yes

No

→ Does your choice satisfy higher education?

Yes → You should be prepared for a higher education course and the career which follows it

STOP

No

Have you ecked ubject eeds or the areer

No ↓
You should be ready for a specific career

No ↓
Check guides

onsult art 2

1 *University Entrance: The Official Guide**
2 *The Polytechnic Courses Handbook**
3 *A Compendium of Higher Education* – full-time and sandwich courses in the 'new' universities, polytechnics and other colleges outside the university sector.

*These publications will be replaced in June 1993 by *University and College Entrance: The Official Guide*

Closing the Doors on Careers

1 Art

If you have low grades in **art** these careers may be closed to you:

Architectural technician work
Architecture
Art and design
Cartography
Landscape architecture.

2 English or English literature

If you have low grades in **English** or **English literature**, these careers may be closed to you:

Accountancy*
Accounting
Actuarial work
Advertising
Air piloting*
Air traffic control*
Army officer*
Astronomy*
Audiology technician
    work
Baking technology
Banking
Beauty therapy
Brewing technology*
Building society work*
Cardiology technician
    work
Chiropody
Civil Service clerical
    assistant
Civil Service clerical
    officer
Civil Service executive
    officer
Company secretaryship*
Customs and excise work
Dental therapy work
Dietetics
Dispensing optics
Environmental health*
Estate agency and
    auctioneering
Exporting

Fashion design and
    production
Forestry
Geology
Health services
    management
Home economics
Horses, work with
Housing management*
Insurance
Interpreting and
    translating
Journalism*
Landscape architecture*
Legal executive work
Legal work – solicitor
Librarianship
Local government
    administration
Marketing
Mathematics
Medical laboratory
    science work
Medical records work*
Merchant Navy deck
    officer and radio officer
Meteorology
Midwifery*
Neurophysiology
    technician work
Nursery nursing
Occupational therapy
Ophthalmic optics

Organisation and
  methods and work
  study
Orthoptics*
Osteopathy*
Personnel work
Photography*
Physiotherapy
Printing technology
Public relations
Purchasing and stock
  control
Radiography/radiotherapy

Recreation
  administration
Royal Air Force officer
Royal Navy officer
Speech therapy*
Surveying
Teaching*
Town planning*
Trading standards
  administration
Travel work
Veterinary nursing work

* English grade C or above required

3 Modern foreign languages

If you have a low grade in a **modern foreign language**,
these careers may be closed to you:

Archive work
Diplomatic Service
Interpreting and translating
Patents
Speech therapy

4 Geography

If you have a low grade in **geography**, these careers may
be closed to you:

Cartography (preferred)
Landscape architecture.

5 Mathematics

If you have a low grade in **mathematics**, these careers
may be closed to you:

Accountancy
Accounting
Actuarial work
Advertising
Air piloting
Air traffic control
Architectural technician work
Architecture
Army officer
Astronomy
Audiology technician work
Baking technology
Banking
Biochemistry
Biology
Brewing technology
Broadcasting (technical)
Building society work
Building technician and technology work
Cardiology technician work
Cartography
Chemistry
Computer-programming
Dentistry
Dietetics
Dispensing optics (or physics)
Design
Economics
Engineering
Environmental health
Estate agency and auctioneering
Fashion design and production
Food science and technology
Forestry
Geology
Health services management
Horticulture
Information science
Insurance
Landscape architecture
Leather technology
Local government administration
Marketing
Market research
Materials science
Mathematics
Medical laboratory science work
Medical records work
Medicine and surgery
Merchant Navy deck officer
Merchant Navy engineering officer
Merchant Navy radio officer
Metallurgy
Meteorology
Midwifery
Neurophysiology technician work
Operational research
Ophthalmic optics

Organisation and methods and work study
Orthoptics
Patents
Personnel work
Pharmacy
Photography
Physics
Plastics and rubber technology
Printing technology
Psychology
Public relations
Purchasing and stock control
Quarrying
Radiography/radiotherapy

Recreation administration
Royal Air Force officer
Royal Navy officer
Speech therapy
Statistics
Surveying
Surveying technician work
Teaching*
Textile technology
Town and country planning
Trading standards administration
Travel work
Veterinary work

*Mathematics grade C or above required

6 Single and double sciences

If you have low grades in **science**, these careers may be closed to you:

Air piloting
Air traffic control
Animal nursing auxiliary
Animal technician work
Archaeology
Architectural technician work
Architecture
Astronomy
Audiology technician work

Baking Technology
Beauty therapy
Biochemistry
Biology
Brewing technology
Broadcasting (technical)
Building technician and technology work
Cardiology technician work
Chemical engineering

Chemistry
Chiropody
Dairy technology
Dental hygiene work
Dental therapy work
Dentistry
Dietetics
Dispensing assistant/pharmacy technician work
Dispensing optics
Dyeing
Engineering
Environmental health
Farming (some levels)
Fashion design and production
Food science and technology
Forestry
Geology
Hairdressing
Home economics
Horticulture
Information science
Laboratory technician work
Landscape architecture
Leather technology
Materials science
Medical laboratory science work
Medicine and surgery
Merchant Navy deck officer
Merchant Navy engineering officer
Merchant Navy radio officer
Metallurgy
Meteorology
Midwifery
Museum work
Nature conservation
Neurophysiology technician work
Nursing
Occupational therapy
Operational research
Ophthalmic optics
Orthoptics
Osteopathy
Patents
Pharmacy
Photography
Physics
Physiotherapy
Printing technology
Psychology
Quarrying
Radiography/radiotherapy
Recreation administration
Speech therapy
Surveying
Surveying technician work
Teaching
Textile technology
Trading standards administration
Veterinary work

Opening Doors to Careers Later

However, there are ways of opening doors to careers later.

1 By sitting special tests or examinations set by employers or professional bodies as alternatives to public exams.

2 Aiming higher than a 16+ entry into a given field, eg graduate entry, which would bypass GCSE required subjects.

3 Mature entry (over 25 years of age). Mature students who apply for a place on a university or training course may not have to satisfy the normal academic requirements. When older people who do not have the normally required number of GCSEs apply for a job, employers will often take their experience into consideration instead. Many careers are open to mature entrants.

Resolving those clashes

If you are forced into a choice you are not happy about, look around for ways of compensating.

For example

Can't take typing?	Look around for evening classes (but make sure you get the head teacher's permission)
Clashes with music?	Try lessons or groups out of school
Art or drama not possible?	How about a school art club or extra-curricular drama?
Language clash?	Are there evening classes?

Some subjects at GCSE are offered again in the sixth form. Others can be bypassed at GCSE but still studied to A-level. There is often more flexibility than first appears.

9 Looking into the Future

The courses you are taking for the next two years should be enjoyable but the exams are not just there for the fun of sitting them. They measure your performance and prepare the way for the next stage.

Think of GCSE grades as keys which will open some doors. The difficulty is that you are not yet sure which doors you will want to open. Therefore you don't know which keys to choose. Obviously the bigger the bunch, the more doors you will be able to open.

Let's start with the doors. There will be four of them facing you in two to four years' time.

We will look at each one in turn and examine the ways of opening it. Then we will take a broad view of the opportunities which lie on the other side.

Sixth-Form Education in School or College

Which subjects may I need if I go on to GCE Advanced level?

You may know already that you want to go on to take your A-levels. You may even know which subjects you would like to take.

Different institutions make different arrangements, though most normally require you to have gained a GCSE grade A to C in order to allow you to take a subject at A-level. Often they prefer you to have gained at least a GCSE grade B to begin an A-level subject. Just occasionally it may not be possible to take a subject at GCSE that you are likely to want to study at A-level. Remember, though, that it is important for everyone to complete a GCSE course in

English, mathematics and a science. Find out from your teachers what happens in your local sixth form or college.

Don't just concentrate on subjects you know you will need at A-level. Later on, a college offering higher education courses (ie at 18+) will want to see evidence of study in breadth and depth, and Key Stage 4 of the National Curriculum should ensure that this occurs. For the future scientists a GCSE grade A to C in a language and the humanities is important now. For those inclined to the humanities, a GCSE grade A to C in science is vital at this stage.

It is important, however, to remember that in some subjects, particularly science and languages, the A-level work follows on from the GCSE work. These are subjects in which you develop your knowledge step by step and they are obviously more difficult to take up again once you have given up on them.

If you don't know what subjects you want to do at A-level, don't worry. There is no need to make up your mind at this stage. The National Curriculum at Key Stage 4 is designed to provide a broad range of GCSE subjects which will give you the chance to decide which ones you might like to study further. You can make the decisions about A/AS-level subjects during Year 11. Some sixth forms, colleges and FE establishments will allow you to read for a combination of A/AS-levels and GCSEs.

Can I Take GCSEs After the Age of 16?

The answer to this question can only be given by individual schools and colleges. Traditionally, sixth forms have been geared to A-levels, but recently sixth-form courses have been designed for 16+ exams, vocational studies and A/AS-levels. Most students are prepared to take their GCSEs at the end of Year 11, some are ready earlier, some later, some may be recommended not to sit them at all. There are people who come back to subjects they dropped at school and sit exams many years later. We don't all develop in the same way or at the same speed. It might be a very good thing to stay on at school into the sixth form for GCSEs. Talk to your teachers; ask their advice. There will also be many post-16 colleges which offer GCSE courses.

In addition, many colleges of FE offer courses at GCSE which are directed in certain areas, such as a pre-business studies GCSE programme, a pre-art and design GCSE programme – and many others centred on a general vocational area. These enable you on completion to have the option to go on to A/AS-levels or to take up a vocational course directly related to a particular area of work and employment.

Resitting

It may be vital for your career plans to resit certain exams in which your grades were not good enough. You may be pleased to know that coursework done for an exam in Year 11 can be offered again for your retake (given that you are satisfied with it). Many students prefer to submit coursework which they have produced during their retake year. (The present trend is for most GCSE subjects to be at most 40% coursework and 60% examination based, though there is a tendency to reduce this to 20% – 80%.)

Warning

- ❗ It is always useful to know you can have a second chance, but don't allow it to lull you into a false sense of security.
- ❗ Retaking some subjects could prevent you studying others because of the way the timetable works.

One reason for continuing at GCSE level after 16 is to gain better grades in subjects which are important to your future but in which you did not fare so well first time round. Another reason is to study new subjects which were not previously offered on your timetable at Key Stage 4.

These new subjects might be:

Health studies
Russian
Photography
Sociology
Psychology
Communication studies
Government, politics and law
Italian
Media studies

Most of these subjects are related to particular career fields. Courses in them can be very useful; they give you the chance to sample the subject and make up your mind whether you want to pursue a career in it.

Some schools and colleges run a one-year post-16 course with experience of work. You spend one day a week or a block of weeks in industry or in a local further

Search

1 Find out what the post-16 arrangements are in your school area.
2 Are there any subjects you must have before you can go on to the next stage?
3 Use your school or college careers library, your careers teacher and your careers officer to help you gain long-term information.

education college gaining industrial experience or beginning a basic, specialist course before leaving full-time education. Many colleges build experience of work into GCSE courses and most students will have had the opportunity of a placement in work, usually of two weeks' duration, during Key Stage 4.

Employers make their own use of GCSE results in the selection of new employees. Not all your GCSE subjects will be relevant to the job you have applied for, but your overall choice of subjects, your grades as well as what sort of person you are will be a very useful guide to a prospective employer. Look at the extract below provided with the permission of Cornhill Insurance.

Getting into Cornhill	**Comment**
Educational Qualifications	
At Cornhill we prefer people with either	
a, a GCE in two subjects at A-level, and two at GCSE-level. These passes must include English	post-16 courses are relevant
	note the essential GCSE levels
or	

b, any three passes in GCE at —— **subject freedom post-16**
A-level
or
c, the National Certificate or
National Diploma in Business —— **an alternative route**
and Finance.

We do, however, realise that
not everybody is able to stay in
full- time education until the age
of 18; or pursue part-time
courses such as the National
Certificate. If you haven't reached
this level you will spend more —— **you *can* get in at 16, *but...***
time in training in Cornhill and
your part-time studies will take a
bit longer. We therefore also
consider applications from
people with at least

d, four subjects at GCSE Grades
A to C, including English and
mathematical subject, which will —— **two subjects are now essential**
enable them to study for the
National Certificate.

These qualifications are linked
to the requirements of the
Chartered Insurance Institute, —— **NB those professional bodies again!**
whose Qualifying Examination is
the professional examination of
the insurance industry. You must
check the acceptability of your
particular subjects from the
Examination Handbook of the
Chartered Insurance Institute,
copies of which are freely

THINKS...

available from the Institute at 31 Hillcrest Road, South Woodford, London E18 2JP.

Two quick points

☛ You may apply before your exam results are known.

☛ Equivalent Scottish qualifications are equally acceptable.

Academic qualifications are not everything –

they just set the minimum educational level required. The different jobs already described make their particular demands but throughout Cornhill it is essential to have a good command of English, both in conversation and on paper. You should not be frightened of figures … but generally it is only simple arithmetic that is required! In a firm with such variety of business it is important to be quick thinking and flexible in your approach. You need to be interested in what is going on around you and have sufficient curiosity to assemble the facts on which to base balanced judgments. Persistence too will help; studying for qualifications part-time is not easy, and you must be well motivated and well organised in order to succeed.

some checking to do

always a good idea

Thank goodness! But that does not mean that a cheerful face and a glib tongue will make up for a woolly brain

Youth Training

In September 1983 the government introduced the Youth Training Scheme (YTS), not just to keep the unemployed busy but to provide training for all young people aged 16+ hoping to go into industry. It is now known as Youth Training (YT) and is, on the one hand designed to give broad vocational training, and on the other, to provide a pool of people with experience of work and skills from which to recruit. Some YT courses will have GCSE entry requirements, so it is not true to say that exams don't matter when there is little work about!

Whichever world of employment you choose, the principle remains the same: employers will use

☛ public examination results
☛ your character reference
☛ your Record of Achievement
  to sift out candidates for interview.

If you are 13, GCSEs may seem to you like the buffers at the end of the line. For many there will be a junction on this line which goes a long way further.

The Years 10 and 11 in secondary school are those in which you are preparing for life at work or as a student in further education. It is therefore important that interests that have grown in the previous years should be allowed to develop in a more specialised way in the final years of compulsory schooling and beyond.

Vocational Courses

As an alternative to GCSEs and A/AS-levels you can, after Year 11, go on to follow a vocational route. This is a programme or course which leads to a qualification linked with a particular area of work (hairdressing and beauty, leisure and tourism, engineering, art and design, science, computing and others).

Vocational qualifications are available at different

levels to match with GCSEs, A/AS-levels and higher education qualifications (degrees and diplomas).

To ensure that vocational qualifications at specific levels can be compared with each other (that is, that they have similar standards) and to help companies recognise the levels, all qualifications relating to work are now becoming National Vocational Qualifications (NVQs). The most used levels for 16+ are levels 2 and 3.

NVQs are set out in the form of 'competencies' – 'can do' statements – and a particular group of competencies become a 'unit'.

Qualifications can be gained either by completing all the units for a whole NVQ or credit can be given for individual units. These credits can be used towards other qualifications or for employment.

(Further information about National Vocational Qualifications can be found in section three of the next chapter in this book–pages 141–142.)

NVQ Levels

NVQ level	Description	Broadly equivalent to	BTEC
5	Profession, Middle management	Higher Education	
4	Higher technician, Junior management	Higher Education	HNC/ HND
3	Technician, Advanced craft, Supervisor	2+ A-levels (or equivalent in AS)	National awards
2	Basic craft	4+ GCSEs A – C awards	First
1	Foundation	Other GCSEs	

Spotlight on BTEC

The Business and Technology Education Council (BTEC) award nationally recognised qualifications other than degrees. The four levels of BTEC qualification are **First, National, Higher National** and **Continuing.**

BTEC First Certificates and Diplomas are designed to develop essential skills and knowledge and to provide a foundation for further study. To enter a BTEC First course you must be at least 16 years-old. Formally no GCSEs are required but you must show evidence of 'an ability to benefit from the course' so many colleges will expect students straight from school to have some GCSEs at grades E and above. The Certificate courses last one year part-time, the Diplomas one year full-time or two years part-time. Courses are available in agriculture; horticulture; business and finance; construction; design; distribution studies; caring; hotel and catering studies; engineering; performing arts; leisure studies and science. The courses are held at colleges of further education. After you have successfully completed a BTEC First course you can either start a job or go on to a BTEC National course. The BTEC First Certificates and Diplomas are at National Vocational Qualification level 2.

BTEC National Certificates and Diplomas are qualifications for technicians and junior administrators. **To enter a course you must be:**
☞ at least 16 **and hold either**
☞ a BTEC First Certificate/Diploma
☞ **or** four GCSEs at grades A, B or C (for certain courses particular subjects are preferred. See the 'Careers Guide' for details.)
☞ **or** 14–16 Foundation Programme with appropriate attainment

The National Certificate courses last two years part-time and the National Diploma courses last two years full-time or three years part-time or sandwich study.

Courses are available in the following occupational areas: built environment (building studies, civil engineering, construction, land administration and surveying), business and finance & public administration; computing and information systems; design; distribution; engineering; hotel and catering; land and countryside (agriculture, floristry, horse studies and horticulture); leisure services; and science and caring. After you have successfully completed a BTEC National award you can either start a job, go on to a BTEC Higher National course or if you achieve good grades go on to a degree course.

BTEC Higher National Certificates and Diplomas are qualifications for higher-technician, managerial and supervisory levels. A student should normally be at least 18 years-old and hold an appropriate BTEC National award or GCSEs and A-levels. The actual requirements depend on the course – some details are given in the 'Careers Guide' on page 160. The Certificate courses last two years part-time; the Diploma courses last two years full-time or three years part-time or sandwich study. Courses are available in the same occupational areas as the BTEC National awards.

BTEC Continuing Education Certificates, Diplomas and Units are for adults wishing to update their skills.

Spotlight on Higher Education

The 18+ stage probably looks a long way off. It is not too early, however, to take a look, if only to check out the relation between **GCSE and University, University/ Polytechnic or Colleges of Higher Education.**

First of all, remember that when you apply for a college or university place, you will be doing it from the first year in the sixth form. You will have started on your A-level or BTEC course but your academic track record will be based on your GCSE qualifications. When you complete your application form they, together with your predicted grades at A/AS-level, are entered as your representatives who will speak on your behalf, so they had better be good!

But 16+ exams have a more precise duty to do as far as universities, university/polytechnics and colleges of higher education are concerned. There are two kinds of qualifications you need to possess:

Entry Qualifications	**+**	**Faculty or Departmental Qualifications**

☞ **Entry qualifications**
These are basic qualifications to be obtained before the university will accept you to study anything.

☞ **Faculty/departmental requirements**
Special subjects relevant to your proposed course of study required by the faculty or department you wish to join. These subjects will vary from department to department.

For Example

You wish to go to Barchester University to read medicine.

University of Barchester

General requirements to study any course at the University	Course requirements for medicine
5 GCSE subjects at grades A, B or C, including English, GCSE mathematics or a science + 2 GCE A-levels	3 A-levels, one in chemistry and two from biology, physics and mathematics. The subject not held at A-level must be held at GCSE grades A, B or C

You must satisfy the requirements in the left-hand column to go to Barchester at all. If you wish to read medicine there, you must also satisfy the particular subjects which the admissions tutor for medical students requires to ensure that all students on the course have good foundations in science which are necessary to progress on the course.

These are the minimum requirements but competition for places is fierce and in practice a school-leaver would be expected to have at least six well-balanced GCSEs at grades A, B, or C taken at one sitting and two good A-levels. The rather low minimum requirements allow universities to take individual circumstances into account.

Generally speaking, the wider your range of subjects, the broader your choice of higher education courses.

The three principal books for consultation are:

Search

☛ for university/polytechnics
The Polytechnic Courses Handbook
Southport Book Distributors Ltd, 12–14 Slaidburn
Crescent, Southport, Merseyside PR9 9YF
☛ for universities
University Entrance: The Official Guide
from Sheed and Ward, 14 Coopers Row, EC3N 2BH
☛ for other colleges of higher education
*Guide to the Colleges and Institutes of Higher
Education* from Mr G R Mann, Administrative
Officer, Standing Conference of Principals, Edge
Hill College of Higher Education, Ormskirk,
Lancashire L39 4QP

A Point to Think About

A degree course is not usually training for a career; it is an
academic education. Many arts graduates' careers have
little connection with their degree subject. For instance, a
history graduate may enter a marketing training scheme
with a large company. They would not be using history
directly at all. Companies often run graduate training
schemes which offer higher starting salaries and better
promotion prospects than a school-leaver could expect.
There are also graduate training schemes in the Civil
Service, the armed services, local government
administration and the police. In some cases a degree
course is training for a specific profession and the
profession is open only to graduates of these courses (for
example, architecture, dentistry, medicine, ophthalmic
optics, pharmacy and veterinary science). However, if you
hold a degree in one of these subjects you do not have to
enter the profession.

10 Supporting Attractions

The education scene is constantly changing. This is as true of the 14 – 16 stages as of any other and there are five developments of which you should be aware. Four have been implemented nationwide and the other can be found in some form or other in many schools. They are all worth thinking about. They are:

1 Youth Training
2 Records of Achievement
3 National Vocational Qualifications
4 Leisure education
5 The National Curriculum, which we have discussed fully in the earlier chapters.

1 Youth Training (YT)

Youth Training is a planned programme of approximately two years' work experience and training. Its aims are to give you competence in a range of skills and the ability to apply your skills in different situations, to have confidence in yourself and your ability and to gain recognised vocational qualifications.

In most parts of the country YT is available in nearly all areas of work, including administrative and office work, health and community care, hairdressing, sales work, science, catering, agricultural work, building, engineering, garage work, printing and others.

YT is open to all 16 and 17 year-old school-leavers and in theory all 16 and 17 year-olds are guaranteed a place on YT. However, in the current economic situation it has proved impossible to place all YT applicants in work. It is a mix of on-and off-the-job training and all programmes must offer young people the opportunity to obtain recognised vocational qualifications to a minimum standard; normally this will be NVQ level 2.

Young people may be either employed or non-employed on YT and many traditional apprenticeships such as those in the building trades, motor mechanics, engineering and hairdressing have been fully integrated within YT. YT has become the usual – and often the only – route into these jobs.

Your local Careers Service office is likely to publish a booklet giving details of YT programmes available in your area. Remember, a weekly trainee allowance is paid to you and this opportunity exists regardless of your gender, race or ability.

Many employers now recruit through YT, some offering fully paid jobs with Youth Training, but others have not joined the scheme and they will continue to offer employment including, in some cases, associated day release for further education. If, at the end of Year 11, you do not intend to continue in full-time education you will need to consider whether it will be better for you to apply for permanent employment immediately or whether you should apply for a YT place.

What are the implications for subjects in Key Stage 4?

☞ Some training will involve complex technical skills, so selection based on school examinations may occur.

☞ Some employers or industrial groups may recruit only those who have been on their training scheme.

☞ Not all who take a training scheme will land a job at the end of it. There is no guarantee of work so get as many qualifications as you can while you are still at school; they will be invaluable.

☞ The old established routes of GCSE/A-levels in school or college will still be available.

☞ The better your 16+ qualifications, the stronger will be your position to choose.

2 Records of Achievement

Examination results do not tell the whole story. People who train and employ school-leavers are no longer satisfied with the rather narrow picture that exam results give–they only indicate academic ability. Of course this is important, but how successful an employee you are likely to be also depends on the kind of person you are.

School reports as we used to know them have mostly been replaced by a profiling system which is done by you as well as your teacher. An example of a young person's Record of Achievement in Mathematics in the first half of Year 10 is shown below.

MANOR COMMUNITY COLLEGE
RECORD OF ACHIEVEMENT

MATHEMATICS

NAME: Laura Prentis 10 MU

COMMUNICATION SKILLS
PUPIL COMMENT: I think that I'm quite a good communicator both orally and in writing. I think that I have understood well all the mathematical language which I have come across so far. I think that my presentation in my work books is quite good.

TEACHER COMMENT: Your progress is excellent with very good results in your last two tests. Your written work is well presented, you are well organised and oral work is very thoughtful.

PROBLEM SOLVING SKILLS
PUPIL COMMENT: I enjoy problem solving because each problem is different. I like the way we have the choice of how to set our work out and our results. ie graphs, tables etc. I find some easy and some hard, I find the harder ones better as they are more of a challenge.

TEACHER COMMENT: Your work in this area is sound. You analysed the task well and were able to use the analysis to solve most of the problem. At the end your work on predicting future behaviour was a bit weak.

AGREED TARGET:
To maintain my present rate of progress.

Laura Prentis   F. Murphy   DATE: 22.01.92.
At the present time, based on our assessment of your attainment, we think you are likely to be entered for G.C.S.E. at the following level:

FOUNDATION ☐   INTERMEDIATE ☐   HIGHER ☑

Thus when completed, your Record of Achievement, whether a local or the National Record of Achievement, is a document you can take with you which highlights your skills and abilities both in and out of school. It should be a help in planning your future since it summarises your achievements at school, your qualifications, your activities, any jobs and experiences of work you have had and a personal statement written by you.

> If you would like further information about the National Record of Achievement ask your teachers or careers adviser or write to:
> The Employment Department
> N705
> Moorfoot
> SHEFFIELD
> S1 4PQ.

☛ Achievement recording is also something you can do. Collect all the evidence from sources in and out of school that have something valuable to say about you.

> **eg**
>
> **music awards**
> **swimming certificates**
> **school commendations**
> **athletic achievements**
> **guide/scout awards**
> **evidence of club membership**
> **first-aid certificates**
> **activity photographs**
> **competition awards**
> **interesting letters**
> **records of special achievements**

Mount everything carefully in a non-stick photograph album and you will have something interesting to take with you when you go for an interview.

3 National Vocational Qualifications

NVQs are about being able to do a job well. They are based on skills and standards of competence which have been set by appropriate industries, by representatives of employers, trade unions and professional groups. Bodies who have previously awarded vocational qualifications, such as City and Guilds, RSA and BTEC are changing their awards to fit the NVQ way of measuring achievement.

Each NVQ is made up of a number of units which set out exactly what you must be able to do and to what standard. A unit is like a mini-qualification. You get an NVQ credit for each unit you complete. You can choose which units you do and qualify at your own speed. Each NVQ has an area of competence and a level to fit it to the NVQ Framework. So, you can progress through 5 levels in the framework. Level 1 is the simplest.

If you work for NVQs you can get your own National Record of Vocational Achievement. The National Record consists of four sections:

The Personal Record
The Action Plan
The Assessment Record
Certificates.

Your National Record should help you to plan your future as well as show what you have already achieved. There are now 250 NVQs. Locally you should be able to gain information from your TEC – Training and Enterprise Council. Guides are also available from NCVQ at 222 Euston Road, London NW1 2BZ (telephone: 071-387 9898).

4 Leisure Education

Sounds like time to put your feet up! Not quite, but there could be periods ahead when you have more time on your hands than you expect.

☞ Unemployment remains a fact of life which will not go away. If there is a time when it is hard to find work, you will have unexpected time to spare.

☞ When a firm runs into difficulties because orders are few, short-week working is sometimes the answer. This can mean weekends which are four days long. Sounds marvellous, but only if you have something useful to do with the time.

☞ Job-sharing is likely to become more common. This means you work half a day and a partner works the other half. This means even more time at your disposal.

☞ The age of retirement is likely to come down and, thanks to medical science, people are living longer – two more reasons why people have more free time.

Your generation may have more leisure time than any previous generation and this could affect your course choices.

Are there subjects which could help you become a more skilful homemaker?

Consider: social studies, cookery, textiles, etc.

Are there subjects which could lead to a club activity?

Consider: drama, music, art, geography, history.

Are there subjects which would enable you to offer a service?

Consider: typing, accounts, office practice.

Are there subjects which would help you care for others?

Consider: home economics, first-aid, biology, community service.

It's a fresh way to look at subject choice and one which could have lasting importance.

Careers books tend to baffle you with abbreviations. Here is a list of the more common ones you are likely to meet.

A-level	A two-year academic course focussed on one subject designed to follow on from GCSEs. Most students take 2–4 A-levels and good grades (A, B, Cs) are the entry requirement for higher education
AS-level	An AS-level is roughly half the work of an A-level
BTEC	Business & Technology Education Council
CDT	Craft, Design, Technology is one of the subjects under the Technology umbrella and a foundation subject
CGLI	City and Guilds of London Institute (an examining body for vocational courses)
CRAC	Careers Research and Advisory Centre
DipHE	Diploma of Higher Education
GCSE	General Certificate of Secondary Education
MFL	Modern Foreign Language
NVQ	National Vocational Qualification
RSA	Royal Society of Arts Examination Board (an examination body for certain vocational courses)
TEC	Training and Enterprise Council
YT	Youth Training

11 Getting Help

No one pretends that it's easy to make decisions about one's future. There are so many unknowns. You won't know if you like a subject, or if you are any good at it, until you've studied it. You can't know exactly which subjects you'll need four years from now.

This is why help is important. Nobody should feel that they have to get on with it by themselves. Most schools have particular staff whose job it is to make sure the issues are clear, and who will spend a good deal of time making sure you know what you are doing.

Different people will give advice from different points of view. It is important to understand their point of view when discussing problems with them.

Who is available to help you with your decisions?

Talk to:

Form teacher or tutor who sees you in an all-round school situation.

Talk to:

Careers officers and careers teachers who give you independent, unbiased advice over the various choices you will have to make.

Talk to:

College staff who can advise upon routes through further education which will enable you to obtain specialist qualifications.

Talk to:

Employers who can offer you advice based upon their experience of business and industry in the light of employment needs and training opportunities.

Talk to:

Subject teachers who provide an objective view of your subject abilities.

Talk to:

Parents who know you best of all as a person.

There will be plenty of things to talk over with them for you will be seeking to achieve a compromise between

☞ what you like
☞ what you are good at
☞ what you are recommended to do
☞ what you need.

What should you discuss with your advisers?

☞ Like

It would be nice if you liked all your school subjects, but probably you don't. Remember that likes and dislikes are often determined by who teaches you. Is it sensible to choose subjects on that basis? You will probably be taught by someone else next year anyway. Is it the way of learning that makes a subject popular? Field work, projects, a visual approach, experiments? What really triggers likes and dislikes?

☞ Good at

Are you good at the things you like? Do you always like the things you are good at? How soon should you specialise in your best subjects? Can this be carried too far? Could you drop some of your good subjects for two years and then take them up again? What are the skills which make you good at a subject anyway?

☞ **Recommended**

Who recommends you to do what? Do your parents and teachers give conflicting advice? How can you sort out objective and subjective viewpoints? Have you a good balance of subjects and methods of working? Are you carrying too many subjects that rely heavily on your memory?

☞ **Need**

How far ahead have you looked? Does your choice allow you sufficient flexibility? What changes might occur in the careers field that interests you? If changes come, will you be able to adapt to them? Where can you get advice on questions like these?

Like

Good at

Your Subject Choice

Need

Recommended

within the framework of what is required

12 Making the Choice

Now comes the crunch. After all the reading, talking, finding out and discussion, the choice has to be made. And only you can make it. You have the information you need; now you just draw it all together. Use the chart overleaf to set out the possibilities.

Using the Chart

On the top of the chart are the main subject families. A well-balanced choice will include subjects from each family. Write in all the subjects you *can* include for Key Stage 4 on the '**Offered**' level.

	English			Science		Modern Foreign Languages		
Offered	English Language	English Literature	Mathematics	Single Science	Double Science	FRENCH		
Required	✓		✓	✓		✓		
Like	✓							
Good at	✓							
Recom'd	✓		✓			✓		
Need	✓		✓					
Final Choice	ENGLISH		MATHS	SCIENCE		FRENCH		

manities		Technology				Creatives			Other	
MODERN STUDIES	CLASSICAL STUDIES					MUSIC				
✓	✓									
	✓									

Along the **'Required'** line, put a tick in each subject box which you are required to do within the National Curriculum.

Against **'Like'** put a tick in the box for every subject you like. Against **'Good at'** tick the subjects you are reasonably good at. Against **'Recommended'** tick the subjects that your teachers have recommended you to take for GCSE. Against **'Need'** tick the GCSE subjects required for any special career you are interested in.

When you have completed the chart look at the overall picture it presents. The pattern of ticks will be a useful guide when you make your final choice.

Footnote 1

We wish you every success both with making your decisions for your Key Stage 4 courses, as well as with the subjects themselves when the courses begin.

We suggest you keep referring to this Student Helpbook
☛ To keep up to date with your thinking about careers by using the information in Part 2
☛ Throughout Key Stage 4.
Michael Smith
Veronica Matthew

Footnote 2

Answer to the outdoor pursuits problems on page 22

The object of the exercise was to achieve a balance between comfort, enjoyment and safety. The more you take, the more comfortable you will be at camp but the more you will regret it during the day. The ideal limit is about 13.5 kg, but note you must be prepared for some unexpected situations. Allowing for the worst possible weather the following choice would be ideal:

rucksack with dustbin liner
sleeping bag
lightweight tent with sewn-in groundsheet
waterproof outer clothing
stove/fuel
matches
survival bag
first-aid kit
emergency rations
spare clothing (perhaps socks and a light tracksuit)
food to last two days
map of the area to be covered
compass
whistle
torch
completed route card
water container

Personal gear to be worn

boots

anorak

sweater

woollen socks

woollen-based trousers (not jeans!)

woollen-based shirt

gloves

Note

If you were to climb Ben Nevis in January, you would need extra and different gear.

13 Where Can I Find Out More?

General

Working In Series. This is the main series of careers booklets published by the Careers and Occupational Information Centre (COIC). After each career in the 'Careers Guide', reading has been recommended and in most cases it includes a booklet in this series. The price quoted in the 'Careers Guide' does not include postage. You will also fine COIC's *Occupations '93* useful to look at. The address to write to is: The Careers and Occupational Information Centre, Sales Department, Moorfoot, Sheffield S1 4PQ.

Equal Opportunities – a Careers Guide by Anna Alston, (consultant editor Ruth Miller) is an excellent general careers book published by Penguin.

The Career Counsellor's Job Book. Published for CRAC by Hobsons Publishing PLC, Bateman Street, Cambridge CB2 1LZ. This annual publication gives details of opportunities offered by British employers to those entering employment from school-leavers at 16 with or without GCSEs to post-graduates. Your careers teacher or co-ordinator should have this.

Decisions at 15/16+. Published for CRAC by Hobsons Publishing PLC, Bateman Street, Cambridge CB2 1LZ. A guide to the decisions facing the 15 year-old.

Decisions at 17/18+. Published for CRAC by Hobsons Publishing PLC, Bateman Street, Cambridge CB2 1LZ. A sixth-former's starting point for thought and discussion with parents, teachers and careers advisers on the range of choice after A-levels.

Excellent free factsheets on BTEC courses are available from the Publications Despatch Unit, Business and Technology Education Council, Central House, Upper Woburn Place, London WC1 0HH (please specify the level of the course you are interested in and the occupational area).

A *Compendium of Higher Education* is a comprehensive guide to advanced full-time and sandwich courses in the new polytechnic/universities, and other colleges outside the university sector. It is published by the London and South East Advisory Council for Education and Training (LASER), 232 Vauxhall Bridge Road, London SW1V 1AU.

The Advisory Councils publish lists of all part-time, sandwich and full-time courses in their area.

East Anglian Regional Advisory Council for Further Education, Looms Lane, Bury St Edmunds IP33 1HE.

East Midlands Further Education Council, Robins Wood House, Robins Wood Road, Aspley, Nottingham NG8 3NH

Northern Council for Further Education, 5 Grosvenor Villas, Grosvenor Road, Newcastle upon Tyne NE2 2RU

North West Regional Association of Education Authorities, Town Hall, Walkden Road, Worsley, Manchester M28 4QE

Southern Regional Council for Education and Training, 26 Bath Road, Reading RG1 6NT

South West Association for Further Education and Training, Bishops Hull House, Bishops Hull, Taunton, Somerset TA1 5RA

West Midlands Advisory Council for Further Education and Training, Mill Wharf, Mill Street, Birmingham B6 4BU

Yorkshire and Humberside Association for Further and Higher Education, Bowling Green Terrace, Jack Lane, Leeds LS11 9SX

Welsh Joint Education Committee, 245 Western Avenue, Llandaff, Cardiff CF5 2YX

University Entrance: The Official Guide. Association of Commonwealth Universities for the Committee of Vice-Chancellors and Principals. Obtainable from Sheed and Ward, 12–14 Coopers Row, London EC3N 2BH.

CRAC Degree Course Guides series. Thirty-five comparative first-degree course guides titled by degree subject; they are revised every two years, half in alternate years. Published for CRAC by Hobsons Publishing.

Directory of Further Education. Comprehensive guide to further education courses leading to formal qualifications in UK polytechnics/universities and other colleges outside the university sector. Published for CRAC by Hobsons Publishing.

The NATFHE Handbook of Initial Teacher Training. Lists courses in education for intending teachers. National Association of Teachers in Further and Higher Education. Obtainable from Linneys Colourprint, 121 Newgate Lane, Mansfield, Nottinghamshire G18 2PA.

Polytechnic Courses Handbook. Lists all the full-time and sandwich courses; published by the Committee of Directors of Polytechnics. Obtainable from Southport Book Distributors Ltd, 12–14 Slaidburn Crescent,

Southport, Merseyside PR9 9YF (covers polytechnic/universities).

Guide to the Colleges and Institutes of Higher Education published by the Standing Conference of Principals. Obtainable from Mr G R Mann, Administrative Officer, Standing Conference of Principals, Edge Hill College of Higher Education, Ormskirk, Lancashire L39 4QP.

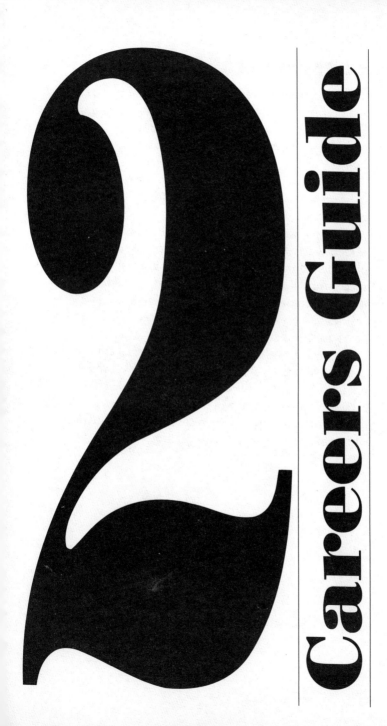

2 Careers Guide

Careers Guide Introduction

This guide is based on a survey of degree and professional requirements that was carried out in June 1992. Entry requirements are changing all the time so it is important to check with the individual colleges and the professional bodies.

Under each career the different entry routes are listed, together with the certificate and diploma courses that can be taken and the GCSEs required.

The phrase 'A good base of GCSEs' is often used for careers where higher education at a university or college of higher education is essential. This normally means that successful candidates will have at least six academic GCSEs at grades A, B or C including English, mathematics, a modern foreign language, science and two other academic subjects.

Many careers listed here have less formal entry routes. You probably have older friends and relatives who have no diplomas and certificates but are doing well in their careers. The routes you will find in the 'Careers Guide' are the authorised ones, and are recommended to anyone who wants to be professionally secure.

Accountancy

An accountant checks the company accounts and advises companies on financial matters such as tax and record-keeping systems. Accountants work in public authorities, companies, or in firms of accountants.

☞ Full-time, sandwich and part-time courses at colleges or by an open-learning or correspondence course for the preliminary, professional and final examinations of the Chartered Association of Certified Accountants. Two A-levels and three GCSEs at grades A,B and C in five distinct subjects are required, including English and mathematics. Only one of the GCSEs may be in a craft subject. Minimum age 18. Three years' relevant accountancy experience is required for candidates for the associateship. The relevant practical experience may be obtained in public practice, industry, commerce, or the public sector. The foundation course is not compulsory.

☞ Study leave to prepare for the examinations of the Institute of Chartered Accountants in England and Wales is provided as part of a training contract with an authorised training office. Most training is available in firms of accountants and increasingly in industrial or commercial organisations. At least two A-levels and three GCSEs at grades A,B or C are required. English and mathematics must be included at either level. All subjects are acceptable. Graduates complete a three-year training contract. Non-graduates usually take a one-year accountancy foundation course at an approved university or higher education college and then spend four years working in an office under a training contract.

☞ Full-time, sandwich and part-time courses at college for all four stages of the examinations of the Chartered Institute of Management Accountants. Three GCSEs at grades A,B or C including English and mathematics and two A-levels are required. All subjects are acceptable.

Candidates for the associateship must be at least 21 and have three years' practical experience.

☛ Full-time, part-time and hybrid courses at college for both foundation and professional examinations of the Chartered Institute of Public Finance and Accountancy for which three GCSEs at grades A, B or C and two A-levels including English and mathematics at either level are required. GCSEs in child development, drama, photography and textiles are not acceptable. The foundation course is compulsory for non-graduates. Those taking the professional examinations must be employed in a financial position by a public authority.

☛ Full-time or part-time college courses for a BTEC National Certificate/Diploma in Business and Finance. Four GCSEs at grades A, B or C preferably including English and mathematics or a BTEC First Certificate/Diploma is required for entry. A BTEC National award is accepted as an alternative to two A-levels for entry to the courses leading to the professional examinations.

☛ Entry after higher education: see Higher Education on page 132. The majority of students entering training to become accountants are graduates.

✍ **Further information** Chartered Association of Certified Accountants, 29 Lincoln's Inn Fields, London WC2A 3EE

Institute of Chartered Accountants in England and Wales, Chartered Accountants' Hall, Moorgate Place, London EC2P 2BJ

Chartered Institute of Management Accountants, 63 Portland Place, London W1N 4AB

Chartered Institute of Public Finance and Accountancy, 3 Robert Street, London WC2N 6BH

📖 **Reading** *Working In* Series: *Accountancy* published by and available from the Careers and Occupational Information Centre, price £2.50

☛ School careers library classification NAB

Accounting Technician Work

Accounting technicians are the support staff on whom the professional accountants rely. In small companies they work on their own, keeping the day-to-day accounts.

☛ Two-year full-time, three-year part-time, open-learning or correspondence courses for the new practical assessments of the Association of Accounting Technicians. These assessments, which test competencies, have replaced the examinations and lead to National Vocational Qualifications (NVQ) at Levels 2–4. There are no fixed entry requirements but you will need to demonstrate that you are both literate and numerate. For candidates direct from school this will mean around four GCSEs at grades A,B or C including English and a numerate subject such as mathematics or principles of accounts.

☛ Two-year full-time or three-year part-time college courses for the BTEC National Certificate/Diploma in Business and Finance followed by study for the Association of Accounting Technicians final examinations. Four GCSEs preferably including English and mathematics or a BTEC First Certificate/Diploma is required for entry to a BTEC course.

In addition a period of approved working experience is required for membership of the Association of Accounting Technicians. Students should register with the Association before starting their course.

✍ **Further information** Association of Accounting Technicians, 154 Clerkenwell Road, London EC1R 5AD

▥ **Reading** *Qualifying as an Accounting Technician* published by and available free from the Association

☛ School careers library classification NAB

Acting
see **Drama**

Actuarial Work

Actuaries apply statistics to life assurance, pension schemes and other insurance problems. For example they might work out the life assurance premiums for different age groups according to their life expectancy.

☛ Correspondence course for the examinations of the Institute of Actuaries while working in an office under a qualified actuary. Three GCSEs at grades A, B or C including English or English literature and two A-levels are required. One of the A-levels must be at least grade B in a mathematical subject or at least grade C in further mathematics or higher mathematics. The other A-levels should be at least grade C. All subjects are acceptable.

☛ Entry after higher education: see Higher Education on page 132. The majority of students entering training to become actuaries are graduates.

✍ **Further information** Institute of Actuaries, Napier House, 4 Worcester Street, Oxford OX1 2AW

▥ **Reading** *Becoming an Actuary* and *What is an Actuary?* published by and available free from the Institute

☛ School careers library classification NAG

Administration
see **Civil Service** *and* **Local Government Administration**

Advertising

After studying the products or services to be advertised, the advertiser will prepare advertisements and place them in newspapers and magazines, on TV and radio as well as on hoardings.

☞ Full-time or part-time college courses for BTEC
National Certificate/Diploma in Business and Finance.
Four GCSEs at grades A, B or C preferably including
English and mathematics or a BTEC First
Certificate/Diploma is required for entry. These can be
followed by either a course for BTEC Higher National
Certificate/Diploma or by study for the CAM certificate.

☞ Two years' part-time evening and home study for
Communication, Advertising and Marketing Education
Foundation (CAM) Certificate in Communication
Studies. The subjects studied are marketing; advertising;
public relations; media; research and behavioural studies;
sales promotion and direct marketing. All students must
be over 18. They must have three GCSEs at grades A, B or
C and two A-levels or five GCSEs at grades A, B or C and
have been employed in a relevant field for one year;
English GCSE must be included, or a BTEC National
Certificate/Diploma in Business and Finance.

☞ Entry after higher education: see Higher Education
on page 132.

✐ **Further information** The Communication
Advertising and Marketing Education Foundation (CAM
Foundation), 15 Wilton Road, London SW1V 1NJ

☞ School careers library classification OD

Aeronautical Engineering
see **Engineering**

Agriculture
see **Farming**

Air Cabin Crew

Air cabin crew look after the needs of passengers on
board a plane, serving meals and selling duty-free goods.
In emergencies it is the responsibility of the cabin crew to
ensure the safe evacuation of passengers.

☛ On-the-job training including a course of several weeks at a training centre. A good general education with some GCSEs, not necessarily at grades A, B or C, is required. Nursing, catering, social welfare or receptionist experience is an advantage. The most useful GCSE subjects are English, geography, mathematics, food and nutrition and foreign languages. Minimum age on most airlines is 20. Candidates have usually had another job before they apply.

✍ **Further information** Aviation Training Association, 125 London Road, High Wycombe, Buckinghamshire HP11 1BT

☛ School careers library classification YAB

Air Force
see **Royal Air Force**

Air Piloting

Pilots are responsible for all aspects of flying an aeroplane. On larger aircraft two or three pilots may work together, sometimes with a flight engineer. Apart from working for airlines, pilots spray crops, make test flights and aerial surveys and give flying instruction.

☛ Full-time courses of approximately 70 weeks at approved training schools at Oxford, Perth, Trent (Cranfield) and the British Aerospace Flying College (Prestwick) for the Commercial Pilot's Licence (Aeroplanes) with Instrument Rating. Nine-month full-time courses at approved training schools at Cranfield, Redhill, Prestwick and Oxford for the Commercial Pilot's Licence (Helicopters). Five GCSEs at grades A, B or C are required, including English, mathematics and a single science award which must include physics. A-levels may be needed for sponsorship.

☛ Entry after higher education: see Higher Education on page 132.

For all courses entrants must be medically fit. Minimum age on qualifying for a professional pilot's licence is 18. The course fees and expenses are over £50,000 unless the student arranges sponsorship.

✍ **Further information** Civil Aviation Authority, FCL4, Aviation House, South Area, Gatwick Airport South, West Sussex RH6 0YR

Aviation Training Association, 125 London Road, High Wycombe, Buckinghamshire HP11 1BT

☛ School careers library classification YAB

Air Traffic Control

Air traffic controllers direct the taking off, landing and movement of air traffic in UK airspace by giving radio messages to pilots while watching aircraft movements on a radar screen.

☛ Two-year college course and on-the-job training for student air traffic controllers. Five GCSEs at grades A, B or C including English and mathematics, and to have studied two A-levels is required. All subjects are acceptable.

✍ **Further information** Civil Aviation Authority Personnel Recruitment Section, Room T820, CAA House, 45–59 Kingsway, London WC2B 6TE

▥ **Reading** *A Career in Air Traffic Control* published by and available free from the Civil Aviation Authority

☛ School careers library classification YAB

Ambulance Service Work

Ambulance crew attend to seriously ill and injured people and give initial medical aid before transporting them to hospital. Their more routine work, patient transport service, includes taking infirm people who cannot use public transport to treatment centres.

☛ On-the-job training with part-time study for examinations. Candidates for entry to the ambulance service must pass a medical test and preference is given to candidates with GCSEs. Minimum age 21, cadets 16 years.

✍ **Further information** Ambulance Service Headquarters, address from the local telephone directory

▥ **Reading** *Working In* Series: *Emergency Services* published by and available from the Careers and Occupational Information Centre, price £2.50

☛ School careers library classification JOC

Animal Nursing
see **Veterinary Nursing**

Animal Technician Work

Animal technicians breed and care for animals in laboratories. They ensure the animals have the highest standards of care. This is a job for people who like working with animals and are interested in science. You cannot do this job unless you love animals but a mature regard for them is needed, not just sentimentality.

☛ On-the-job training with day-release for the Institute's examinations. A GCSE at any grade in a subject demonstrating facility in English and a GCSE at grades A, B or C in mathematics or a science subject or BTEC units in these subjects are required.

☛ Part-time study while employed in a laboratory for the BTEC National Certificate in science (animal technology options). Four GCSEs at grades A, B or C including mathematics and a science subject or a BTEC First Certificate/Diploma is required for entry.

✍ **Further information** Institute of Animal Technology, 5 South Parade, Summertown, Oxford ox2 7jl

▥ **Reading** *Working in* Series: *Animals – Work With* published by and available from the Careers and Occupational Information Centre, price £2.65

☛ School careers library classification WAL

Antique Dealing
see **Retail**

Archaeology

Archaeologists study past people by the scientific analysis of material remains. These remains can be very varied, they may be prehistoric burial mounds, Roman forts, medieval villages and World War II defences.

☛ Higher education is virtually essential for entry; see Higher Education on page 132. Useful GCSEs include foreign languages, history, geography, chemistry and other science subjects, and mathematics. There is some work for which higher education is not required but this is rarely a long-term career.

✍ **Further information** Council for British Archaeology, 112 Kennington Road, London SE11 6RE Council for British Archaeology, Northern Office, King's Manor, York YO1 2EP

▥ **Reading** *Careers in Archaeology* published by and available free from the Council for British Archaeology, please send a large stamped addressed envelope

☛ School careers library classification FAG

Architectural Technician Work

Architectural technicians work closely with architects and other members of the building team. Their work involves preparing working drawings, making surveys, collecting information, inspecting work at a building site and applying computer-aided-design techniques.

☛ Three-year part-time course for the BTEC National Certificate in Building Studies. Four GCSEs at grades A, B or C preferably including science, mathematics and a subject testing command of English or a BTEC First Certificate/Diploma in construction is required for entry.

☛ To become a full member of the British Institute of Architectural Technicians the BTEC National Certificate should be followed by the BTEC Higher National Certificate in Building Studies (Architectural) and then two years of practice qualification.

✍ **Further information** British Institute of Architectural Technicians, 397 City Road, London EC1V 1NE

▥ **Reading** Careers leaflets published by and available free from the Institute

☛ School careers library classification UB

Architecture

Architects design buildings, they must consider the technical specifications as well as the final appearance of the building.

☛ An architect cannot practise in the UK without registering with the Architects' Registration Council of the United Kingdom (ARCUK). Higher education is essential (see Higher Education on page 132). RIBA guidance for minimum requirements is three GCSEs at grades A, B or C including English, mathematics and single award science and at least two A-levels. The two A-levels must be in academic subjects and some colleges specify mathematics. Some aptitude for drawing is required and colleges usually wish to see a portfolio, although GCSE or A-level art is not generally formally required.

✍ **Further information** Royal Institute of British Architects (RIBA), 66 Portland Place, London W1N 4AD

▥ **Reading** *A Career in Architecture* published by and available free from the Royal Institute of British Architects *Architecture, Landscape Architecture and Planning Degree Course Guide*, published for CRAC by Hobsons Publishing PLC, price £5.95

☛ School careers library classification UB

Archive Work

Archivists maintain collections of documents in record offices run by local authorities, central government and a variety of private and other institutions.

☛ Higher education is essential; all the entrants are graduates from a variety of degree subjects; a postgraduate diploma in archive administration is essential. GCSEs in subjects such as history, geography, modern languages and Latin are useful. See Higher Education on page 132.

✍ **Further information** Society of Archivists, Information House, 20–24 Old Street, London EC1V 9AP

⋔ **Reading** *Archives as a Career* published by and available free from the Society of Archivists

☛ School careers library classification FAG

Army

National defence is the main task of all branches of HM Forces. Today's Army is trained in the use of the most sophisticated weapons and equipment.

Officer Entry (Men and Women)

☛ Scholarship scheme for sixth-form study at schools with facilities for A-level studies. Age limits 16 years–16 years 6 months.

☛ Welbeck College provides a two-year sixth-form science-based course preparing boys for a regular commission in a Technical Corps. Candidates must have at least five GCSEs at grades A, B or C including English, mathematics, and double award science. Age limits 15 years 9 months–17 years 6 months.

☛ Regular Commissions: three GCSEs at grades A, B or C and two A-levels are required including, at either level, English, mathematics and either single award science or a foreign language. Age limits $17^3/_4$–25. (Some corps requiring specialist qualifications will accept candidates up to 27.)

☛ Short Service Commissions: five GCSEs at grades A, B or C including English required. Certain subjects are required for technical arms. Age limits $17^3/_4$–25. (Some corps requiring specialist qualifications will accept candidates up to 27.)

☛ Graduate-entry officers may be awarded Regular Commissions or Short Service Commissions. See Higher Education on page 132. The Army can award cadetships to students in higher education; there is also a bursary scheme.

Adult Soldiers

☛ Any fit British subject who passes certain selection tests can serve as a soldier. Age range 17–25.

Junior Entry

☛ Entry as apprentices, junior bandsmen, and junior leaders, the upper age limit is $17^1/_2$. Certain selection tests must be passed.

✎ **Further information** For officer entry: DAR1, Ministry of Defence, Empress State Building, Lillie Road, London sw6 1TR

For soldier and junior entry: DAR2, Ministry of Defence (address as above)

📖 **Reading** A range of publications is available from Army Careers Information Offices

☛ School careers library classification Officers BAF Soldiers BAG

Art and Design

The demand for full-time artists who produce sculpture, paintings and limited editions of prints is extremely small. Designers, however, apply their creative ability to develop a wide range of products. Some designers such as silversmiths, potters and jewellers also work as craftspeople making their own products, while other designers work as part of a team for the mass production of furniture, ceramics, electrical equipment, clothing, footwear and textiles. Other designers create exhibitions, displays and all types of printed material.

Degree Courses

☛ Degree courses in art or design last three years and students specialise in graphic design, three-dimensional design, fine art or textile/fashion design. It is possible to specialise within three-dimensional design: taking industrial design (engineering), furniture, ceramics, interior design or theatre design. Students with three GCSEs at grades A, B or C and two A-levels or with one GCSE at grade A, B or C and three A-levels can enter the degree course without taking a one-year foundation course. A foundation course, however, is recommended for all students.

Non-degree Courses

☛ Two-year full-time or equivalent part-time college programme for the BTEC National Certificate/Diploma in Design. Four GCSEs at grades A, B or C or a BTEC First Certificate/Diploma in Design is required for entry. Students will have to show samples of practical work displaying evidence of potential practical and creative ability.

☛ Two-year full-time or equivalent part-time programme for the BTEC Higher National Certificate/Diploma in Design. For entry either a BTEC National Certificate/Diploma in Design or a foundation course or, exceptionally, one A-level is required.

☛ Vocational courses, which last from one to four years, are available in a wide variety of subjects and entrance requirements vary from evidence of a good general education to the possession of up to five GCSEs at grades A, B or C. For many vocational courses a year's foundation course is not necessary. Vocational courses lead to college diplomas, City and Guilds certificates or professional qualifications such as those of the British Display Society.

☛ Two-year full-time course for the National Diploma advanced level of the British Display Society in either retail display or point of sale, exhibition, prestige and services followed by a year's practical employment and the final level examination of the Society. Three GCSEs at grades A, B or C are required including one subject that gives evidence of the use of English. Candidates must also submit evidence demonstrating potential practical and imaginative ability. All subjects are acceptable. The British Display Society offers BTEC National Diploma and Higher National Diploma holders special category membership.

✍ **Further information** The Design Council, 28 Haymarket, London SW1Y 4SU (not careers in fine art)
British Display Society, 70A Crayford High Street, Dartford, Kent DA1 4EF (display and promotional design only)
National Society for Education in Art and Design (NSEAD), The Gatehouse, Corsham Court, Corsham, Wiltshire SN13 0BZ

▥ **Reading** *Careers in Design*, published by and available free from the Design Council, please enclose a large stamped addressed envelope
Design Courses in Britain also published by the Design Council, price £6.95
Guide to Courses and Careers in Art, Craft and Design published by and available from NSEAD, price £12.15 including postage
Working In Series: *Art and Design* published by and available from COIC, price £2.50
☛ School careers library classification E

Astronomy

Astronomers study the planets, stars and galaxies by applying physics, chemistry, biology, meteorology and many other disciplines.

☞ A degree in astronomy or a closely related subject is essential. A good base of GCSEs which will enable you to take mathematics and physics at A-level is recommended. See Higher Education on page 132.

✍ **Further information** Education Committee, British Astronomical Association, Burlington House, Piccadilly, London w1v 9ag

▥ **Reading** *Becoming a Professional Astronomer* published by the British Astronomical Association, price 40 pence including postage

☞ School careers library classification QOF

Auctioneering
see **Estate Agency**

Audiology Technican Work

Audiology technicians perform a wide variety of tests of hearing and fit and maintain hearing aids.

☞ Two-year part-time course leading to the BTEC National Certificate in physiological measurement while working in the health service. Four GCSEs including English, mathematics and double award science are required.

✍ **Further information** British Association of Audiology Technicians, Mrs M Marshall, Cottage Street Hearing Centre, Brierly Hill, West Midlands dy5 1re

▥ **Reading** *Employment and Training of Audiology Technicians* published by and available free from the British Association of Audiology Technicians – please send a large stamped addressed envelope

Baking Technology

Baking technologists apply their scientific training to the preparation, storage and selling of biscuits, cakes, pies and bread.

☛ Full-time or part-time college courses for the BTEC National Certificate/Diploma in Science (Baking Technology). Four GCSEs at grades A, B or C preferably including at least a single award science, mathematics and a subject testing command of English is required for entry.

☛ Entry after higher education: See Higher Education on page 132.

✍ **Further information** Federation of Bakers, 20 Bedford Square, London WC1N 4AA

☛ School careers library classification SAB

Banking

The high street banks run accounts and the system of cheques. They give advice on investments and promote trade by giving loans and overdrafts. Their other services include foreign exchange and help with financial matters when someone dies. The merchant banks mainly deal with finance for companies.

Discussions are taking place about a merger between the Chartered Institute of Bankers and the Chartered Building Societies Institute.

☛ Part-time courses for the BTEC National Certificate/Diploma in Business and Finance while working in a bank. Four GCSEs at grades A, B or C including English and preferably mathematics or a BTEC First Certificate/Diploma is required for entry.

☛ Part-time study for the three-year Chartered Institute of Bankers' Banking Certificate while working in a financial institution. No entry qualifications are required for the preliminary section (one year); for the final section the candidates must have passed three papers in the preliminary section or hold one or more A-levels or its equivalent and English GCSE at grades A, B or C. Arrangements can be made at schools for pupils in the senior classes to study and sit the examinations of the preliminary section of the

Banking Certificate using Computer Assisted Learning
Packages.

☞ Part-time study for the one-year Chartered Institute
of Bankers' pre-Associateship course. At least one A-level
and GCSE English is required for entry.

☞ The BTEC courses, the Banking Certificate and the
pre-Associateship course can be followed by study for the
Chartered Institute of Bankers' Associateship examinations.

☞ Entry after higher education: see Higher Education
on page 132.

✍ **Further information** The Chartered Institute of
Bankers, 10 Lombard Street, London EC3V 9AS (for
information on the Computer Assisted Learning Packages
phone CAL Department Tel: 0227 762600)

▥ **Reading** *Working In* Series: *Money Business* published
by and available from the Careers and Occupational
Information Centre, price £2.50

☞ School careers library classification NAD

Barrister, the Bar
see **Legal Work**

Beauty Therapy and Consultancy

Beauty therapists treat both the face and the body. They
may give facials or massage customers and remove
unwanted hair by wax or by electrolysis. Beauty
consultants work in shops helping customers to choose
cosmetics.

Beauty Therapists

☞ Full-time and part-time courses for which three to
five GCSEs at grades A, B or C including English and at
least single award science are generally required. For some
courses one A-level is also required. Minimum age is
usually 18.

Beauty Consultants

☛ On-the-job training while working in a department store or for a cosmetic company. Some GCSE subjects (not necessarily at grades A, B or C) are sometimes required. English and mathematics are particularly useful subjects.

☛ Full-time and part-time courses for which two GCSEs at grades A, B or C are generally required.

▥ **Reading** *Working In* Series: *Hairdressing and Beauty* published by and available from the Careers and Occupational Information Centre, price £2.35

☛ School careers library classification IL

Biochemistry

Biochemists usually work in laboratories studying the chemistry of living things. They can work in the food and drug industries, in agricultural and medical research and in hospitals.

☛ Entry after higher education: see Higher Education on page 132. A good base of GCSEs at grades A, B or C will be required for future specialisation in science A-levels.

   For entry as a biochemistry technician see Laboratory technician work

✍ **Further information** Biochemical Society, 59 Portland Place, London W1N 3AJ

▥ **Reading** *Careers for Biochemists* published by and single copies available free from the Biochemical Society *Biochemistry Degree Course Guide* published by Hobsons Publishing PLC, price £5.95

☛ School careers library classification QOM

Biology

Biologists study plants, animals and micro-organisms.

☛ Part-time, sandwich or full-time college courses for

the BTEC National Certificate/Diploma in Science
(Applied Biology). Four GCSEs at grades A, B or C
preferably including double award science, mathematics
and a subject testing command of English or a BTEC First
Certificate/Diploma in Science is required for entry.
☛ Part-time, sandwich or full-time college courses for
the BTEC Higher National Certificate/Diploma.
Applicants must hold a BTEC National
Certificate/Diploma in Science with certain units or
having studied biology and either chemistry or a physical
science to A-level and passed in one of these.
☛ If from the outset you are planning to be a
professional biologist you should aim to take a degree
course. A good range of GCSEs at grades A, B or C
including mathematics and double award science is
required with A-levels in science subjects.
✍ **Further information** Education Department,
Institute of Biology, 20 Queensberry Place, London
SW7 2DZ
📖 **Reading** *Careers with Biology* published by and
available from the Institute of Biology, price £2.90
including postage. Career leaflets are obtainable free from
the Institute provided a large stamped addressed envelope
is sent
Biological Sciences Degree Course Guide published by
Hobsons Publishing PLC, price £5.95
☛ School careers library classification QOD

Bookbinding
see **Printing – Printing Crafts**

Bookselling
see **Retail and Wholesale Distribution**

Botany
see **Biology**

Brewing Technology

Brewing technologists are in charge of the biological processes of malting barley and brewing beer.

☛ Part-time, sandwich or full-time college courses for the BTEC National Certificate/Diploma in chemistry or biology. Four GCSEs at grades A, B or C including mathematics and preferably a double award science or a BTEC First Certificate/Diploma in Science is required for entry.

☛ Part-time, sandwich or full-time courses for the BTEC Higher National Certificate/Diploma in chemistry or applied biology. For the chemistry courses candidates must hold a BTEC National Certificate/Diploma with certain relevant units or A-level chemistry and evidence of substantial study beyond GCSE of mathematics and physics. For the biology courses candidates must hold a BTEC National Certificate/Diploma with certain relevant units or have studied biology and either chemistry or a physical science to A-level and have passed in one of these.

☛ Part-time study for the examinations of the Institute of Brewing. Three GCSEs at grades A, B or C which must include English and mathematics and two science A-levels are normally required from candidates who have had an English education.

☛ Entry after higher education: see Higher Education on page 132. The most suitable degree courses would be in biochemistry, biology, chemistry or chemical engineering. There are a few specialised degree and postgraduate courses in brewing science. A good base of GCSEs at grades A, B or C is required for specialisation in subjects such as mathematics, chemistry and physics or biology at A-level.

✍ **Further information** The Institute of Brewing, 33 Clarges Street, London W1Y 8EE

☛ School careers library classification SAB

Bricklaying
see **Building Crafts**

Broadcasting: Radio and Television

There are many careers in the BBC and the commercial television companies that are dealt with elsewhere in this book – careers such as library work, computing, graphic design, film and video producing, secretarial work and hairdressing. On the technical side of broadcasting there are technical operators and engineers.

Technical operators are divided into three main categories: (i) sound; (ii) camera; and (iii) post-production recording operators. There are also some jobs that are multi-discipline, eg news and current affairs technical operators. GCSE standard in mathematics, science and English is required. Equally important is a genuine interest in and knowledge of a relevant area, eg microphones, tape recorders, photography and the visual arts. All applicants must be over 18 and have normal hearing and colour vision.

Trainee engineers, training to become engineers, service and repair the technical equipment. The minimum requirement is three GCSEs at grades A, B or C in mathematics, science and English; and mathematics and physics studied to A-level or a BTEC National Certificate/Diploma in electronic engineering. A practical interest in electronics is an advantage. Applicants should be over 18 with normal hearing and colour vision. The BBC also recruits a number of graduates each year with non-technical degrees to follow a training programme similar to that of the trainee engineer. Applicants must have GCSE mathematics at grades A, B or C.

Engineers usually have qualifications in electrical engineering or in telecommunications. They have either been trainee engineers or enter with a BTEC Higher

National Certificate/Diploma or a university or college of
higher education degree (see Engineering).

Production work generally requires applicants to have
relevant experience; this can include journalism, the arts,
or theatre. Although no specific qualifications are
requested, most applicants have a good track record
educationally and a strong interest in radio and television
output. Educational subject choice can be as wide as the
topics that fill radio and TV programmes! Increasingly
jobs are advertised on a short-term contract basis (three
months – a year). Competition for jobs is keen.

The BBC offers a limited number of training
opportunities in production and journalism. Jobs and
training opportunities open to newcomers are advertised
in the national press and a summary appears on CEEFAX
page 696.

✍ **Further information** BBC Corporate Recruitment
Services, PO Box 7000, London w12 7zy
BBC Engineering and Technical Operations Recruitment,
201 Wood Lane, London w12 7ts
Commercial television companies: for addresses see
telephone directories

📖 **Reading** *Working In* Series: *TV and Video* published
by and available from the Careers and Occupational
Information Centre, price £1.95

☛ School careers library classification GAL

Building Crafts

Bricklayers build walls with bricks and blocks using a
trowel and mortar.

Carpenters and joiners work with wood, making and
fitting doors, window frames, staircases and floorboards.
Many items are made in a factory nowadays and fitted on
site.

Heating and ventilating workers install heating and air
conditioning systems, mainly in factories and office blocks.

Painters and decorators paint inside and outside a building and put up wallpaper.

Plasterers prepare and apply plaster to inside walls and ceilings. Sometimes they also apply renderings to outside walls.

Plumbers put water systems in new buildings as well as repairing them in existing buildings. Sometimes they install heating systems in houses.

Thermal insulation workers lay mineral wool in the roof and lag pipes (this is often carried out by other craftspeople).

Wall and floor tilers fix tiles to the floors and walls inside buildings.

Roof tilers and slaters fix tiles and slates to roofs after covering the rafters with roofing felt.

In many small building firms a building craftsman or woman undertakes a number of different crafts.

☛ No requirements are laid down nationally but many employers will give preference to candidates with GCSEs at grade E or above in English, mathematics, science and technology for their apprenticeship vacancies.

☛ The Construction Industry Training Board is the principal managing agent for the construction industry for the Youth Training (YT) Scheme. To a large extent YT has replaced the apprenticeship entry to building crafts. Training will take place in a college or training centre as well as at the workplace. Trainees will work towards the new National Vocational Qualifications (NVQ) as they become available.

✍ **Further information** Careers Advisory Service, Construction Industry Training Board, Bircham Newton, King's Lynn, Norfolk PE31 6RH

▥ Reading *Careers in Construction* is published by and available free from the Construction Industry Training Board

Working In Series: *Construction* published by and available from the Careers and Occupational Information Centre, price £2.35

☛ School careers library classification UF

Building Society Work

Building societies lend money on mortgage to people who wish to buy their own homes. They also maintain accounts in a similar way to bank accounts but are not members of the cheque clearing system. Individual building societies lay down their own entry qualifications. If you want to take professional examinations you must follow one of the routes below.

Discussions are taking place about a merger between the Chartered Institute of Bankers and the Chartered Building Societies Institute.

☛ Part-time or correspondence course for the Certificate in Financial Services Practice. There are no formal entry requirements. The Certificate is a qualification for clerical staff or it can be followed by study for the Associateship.

☛ Full-time, part-time or sandwich courses for the BTEC National Certificate/Diploma in Business and Finance. Four GCSEs at grades A, B or C including English and mathematics or a BTEC First Certificate/Diploma is required for entry. This should be followed by study for the Associateship.

☛ Part-time course or a correspondence course provided by the Institute for the Associateship examination of the Chartered Building Societies Institute. Candidates can enter the course with either BTEC National awards in Business and Finance provided certain units are held, or with four GCSEs grades A, B or C including English and mathematics and two A-levels. All GCSE subjects are acceptable. Exemptions from some subjects are given to BTEC Higher National award holders and candidates with degrees.

☛ Entry after higher education: see Higher Education on page 132. Any degree subject is acceptable.

✍ **Further information** The Chartered Building

Societies Institute, 19 Baldock Street, Ware, Hertfordshire
SG12 9DH

📖 **Reading** *Working In* Series: *Money Business* published
by and available from the Careers and Occupational
Information Centre, price £2.50

Building a Career with Building Societies published by and
available free from the Institute

☛ School careers library classification NAF

Building Surveying
see **Surveying**

Building Technician and Technologist Work

Building technicians and technologists work in the offices
of larger building companies and on building sites. They
supervise the work, co-ordinating the various types of
craft worker, ensuring that deadlines are respected and
standards are maintained.

☛ Full-time, part-time and sandwich college courses for
the BTEC National Certificate/Diploma in building
studies. Four GCSEs at grades A, B or C or a BTEC First
Certificate/Diploma in Construction is required for entry.

☛ Full-time, part-time or sandwich courses for the
BTEC Higher National Diploma/Certificate in Building
Studies. Entrants should either have a BTEC National
Diploma/Certificate or four GCSEs at grades A, B or C
including mathematics, a double award science and a
subject testing command of English, and mathematics
and physics studied to A-level with a pass in either. The
BTEC Higher awards and appropriate experience can lead
to associate membership of the Chartered Institute of
Building.

☛ Part-time study for the examinations of the
Construction Surveyors' Institute. Four GCSEs at grades
A, B or C are required. Mathematics, English and at least

a single award science are the preferred subjects. Students should be in approved employment and/or following an approved course.

☛ Entry after higher education: see Higher Education on page 132. Degrees in building are often four-year sandwich courses and require a good base of GCSEs at grades A, B or C for specialisation in mathematics and physical sciences at A-level. Degree holders with appropriate experience can apply to become members of the Chartered Institute of Building.

✍ **Further information** Careers Advisory Service, Construction Industry Training Board, Bircham Newton, King's Lynn, Norfolk PE31 6RH

Chartered Institute of Building, Englemere, Kings Ride, Ascot, Berkshire SL5 8BJ

Construction Surveyors' Institute, Wellington House, 203 Lordship Lane, London SE22 8HA

▥ **Reading** A range of booklets is published by and available free from the Construction Industry Training Board

☛ School careers library classification UD

Butchery
see **Retail and Wholesale Distribution**

Buying
see **Retail and Wholesale Distribution**

Cardiology Technician Work

Cardiology technicians set up and operate equipment for diagnosing and treating heart disease. They often operate machines which produce an ECG (electrocardiogram) of a patient. They are present during open heart surgery and cardiac pacing providing records and measurements for the physician or surgeon.

☛ Two-year part-time day-release or block-release courses for the BTEC National Certificate in science with physiological measurement options. Four GCSEs at grades A, B or C are required for entry including English, mathematics and at least a single award science. This may be followed by the BTEC Higher National Certificate in physiological measurement.

✍ **Further information** Society of Cardiological Technicians, 2 Poplar Avenue, Windlesham, Surrey GU20 6PL

📖 **Reading** *Medical Technical Officers & Assistants (HSC13)* published by the Department of Health and available free from Health Service Careers, PO Box 204, London SE5 7ES

☛ School careers library classification JOB

Careers Work

Careers officers advise young people and adults on their choice of career, training opportunities and further education courses.

☛ One-year or two-year part-time training courses for people with suitable experience in teaching, industry, commerce, social work or public administration. Places at training centres are normally awarded only to those who hold recognised professional qualifications or a degree or who have had five years' relevant experience and meet the academic standard.

✍ **Further information** The Local Government Management Board, Arndale House, Arndale Centre, Luton LU1 2TS

Institute of Careers Guidance, 27a Lower High Street, Stourbridge, West Midlands DY8 1TA

📖 **Reading** *A Career as a Careers Officer* and *Training for the Careers Service* available free from the Institute of Careers Guidance

☞ School careers library classification KED

Carpentry
see **Building Crafts**

Cartography

Cartographers prepare maps from information provided by land surveyors and are increasingly able to make detailed interpretation from aerial photographs and remotely sensed imagery. Most of the posts are in the Ordnance Survey, other government departments or with local authorities, a few with commercial map publishers and the exploration departments of oil companies. The career is in the process of rapid change with the increasing use of computers and geographical information systems.

☞ Day-release courses for the BTEC National Certificate/Diploma in Surveying (Cartography). Four GCSEs at grades A, B or C or a BTEC First Certificate/Diploma is required for entry. The BTEC National awards can be followed by the BTEC Higher National Certificate/Diploma.

☞ Entry after higher education: see Higher Education on page 132. Some degree courses in geography include cartography. Entry requirements are a good base of GCSEs at grades A, B or C preferably including mathematics, a science and a foreign language leading to A-levels including geography and mathematics. Mathematics, computer science and engineering graduates may also be recruited for cartography.

✍ **Further information** Establishment Officer, Ordnance Survey, Romsey Road, Southampton SO9 4DH

▥ **Reading** *Careers in Cartography* single copies available free from R W Anson, Principal Lecturer in Cartography, Oxford Brookes, Gipsy Lane, Headington, Oxford OX3 OBP provided a large stamped addressed envelope is sent

☞ School careers library classification UT

Catering including Hotel and Institutional Management

Caterers prepare and serve food in hotels, restaurants, factories, schools and colleges.

Institutional managers provide food and accommodation in hostels, college halls of residence and similar places.

Hotel managers run hotels and restaurants.

Management and Supervisory Posts

☞ Full-time and part-time college courses for a BTEC National Certificate/Diploma in Hotel, Catering and Institutional Operations. Four GCSEs at grades A, B, or C or a BTEC First Certificate/Diploma is required for entry. The BTEC national awards can be followed by the BTEC Higher National Certificate/Diploma. The Higher award courses can also be entered with three GCSEs at grades A, B, or C and one A-level including English or a subject testing command of English and either mathematics or a subject testing numeracy or a biological or physical science.

☞ Two-year part-time course for the Hotel, Catering and Institutional Management Association's (HCIMA) Certificate. Four GCSEs at grades A, B or C are required including a subject testing command in English and a subject such as mathematics demonstrating numeracy. At least a single award science would be desirable. The BTEC National awards or the Certificate can be followed by a one-year full-time sandwich or three-year part-time or distance learning course for the HCIMA's Diploma. Corporate membership of the HCIMA is open to those who have passed the Diploma examination or an equivalent and have had two years' appropriate experience.

☞ Entry after higher education: see Higher Education on page 132. Several universities and colleges of higher education run degree courses in hotel and catering management. The entry requirements vary but it would be advisable to include in your GCSE subjects English, French, mathematics and double award science.

Hotel Reception, Cookery, Domestic Service and Allied Careers

☛ Full-time and part-time college courses leading to National Vocational Qualifications (NVQ) in housekeeping, reception, food preparation and cooking, food and drink service, etc. The Hotel and Catering Training Company provides training programmes leading to NVQ in a variety of different careers. Some colleges require GCSEs with at least grade D or E in some subjects.

✍ **Further information** Hotel, Catering and Institutional Management Association, 191 Trinity Road, London SW17 7HN

Hotel and Catering Training Company (HCTC), International House, High Street, Ealing, London W5 5DB

📖 **Reading** *Working in the Hotel and Catering Industry* published by HCTC and Macmillans, price £7.99

Working In Series: *Hotel and Catering* published by and available from the Careers and Occupational Information Centre, price £2.65

☛ School careers library classification IB

Ceramics
see **Art and Design**

Ceramics Technology
see **Materials Science and Metallurgy**

Chemical Engineering
see **Engineering**

Chemistry

A chemist studies the elements which compose all matter, applying his knowledge to fields as diverse as synthetic fibres, fertilisers and pharmaceuticals. One word of warning: the person who works in a chemist's shop, preparing drugs, is a pharmacist and not a chemist!

☛ Full-time or part-time college courses for a BTEC National Certificate/Diploma in Science. Four GCSEs at grades A, B or C including mathematics and preferably double award science or a BTEC First Certificate/Diploma in Science is required for entry. Possession of a BTEC National Certificate or Diploma would lead to technician posts.

☛ Three-year sandwich or two-year full-time course for the BTEC Higher National Diploma in Science (Chemistry). An A-level in chemistry and evidence of substantial study beyond GCSE level of a related subject (colleges would normally expect this subject to be mathematics or physics) or a BTEC National Diploma/Certificate with specified units is required for entry. Eligible students on a BTEC Higher National Diploma course may elect to take an additional paper for Graduate Membership Part I of the Royal Society of Chemistry. This may be followed by study for the Part II examinations of the Society.

☛ Most professional chemists have taken a degree in chemistry. See Higher Education on page 132. A good base of GCSEs at grades A, B or C is required and A-levels in mathematics, chemistry and physics should be taken, although some flexibility in A-level subjects is allowed.

✍ **Further information** Royal Society of Chemistry, Burlington House, Piccadilly, London WIV OBN

▥ **Reading** Chemistry – Life beyond Exams published by and single copies available free from the Royal Society of Chemistry

Chemistry Degree Course Guide published by and available from Hobsons Publishing PLC, price £5.95

☛ School careers library classification QOB

Chiropody

Podiatry is gradually replacing the term 'chiropody'. Foot problems affect about three-quarters of the population and podiatrists provide specialist foot care and advice, working in the NHS in hospitals and health clinics and in their own private surgeries. They deal with: children's foot problems, sports injuries, foot deformities, foot care for the elderly and the care of patients with rheumatoid arthritis or diabetes.

☛ Three- or four-year full-time degree course at a university or college of higher education. A good base of GCSEs at grades A, B or C including English and two A-levels including one science subject are normally required.

✍ **Further information** Society of Chiropodists, 53 Welbeck Street, London W1M 7HE
Institute of Chiropodists, 91 Lord Street, Southport, Merseyside PR8 1SA

☛ School careers library classification JAT

Civil Engineering
see **Engineering**

Civil Service

Some civil servants work directly for government ministers, researching and advising on the formulation of policy. The majority work in head or local offices applying this policy. Departments such as the Department of Employment, the Department for Education, the Home Office and the Foreign Office all employ civil servants at executive, administrative and clerical grades. There are also professional, scientific and technical posts in the Civil Service, such as those held by librarians, cartographers, meteorologists and air traffic controllers, which are dealt with under the relevant headings elsewhere in this Careers Guide. Civil service departments are being separated from the main Civil Service and are being set up as independent agencies. They are carrying out their own recruitment and setting their own entry requirements. All branches of the Civil Service carry out their own recruitment at clerical and executive officer level now. The position is changing rapidly and up-to-date information should be obtained from your local Jobcentre or careers office.

Administrative trainees (including equivalent posts in the Diplomatic Service) – the 'Fast stream'
☛ A good base of GCSEs at grades A, B or C is required; an honours or postgraduate degree is essential as competition is very keen. (See Higher Education on page 132.)

Executive Officer
☛ There are no longer any nationally applied requirements but agencies will normally be recruiting candidates with three GCSEs including English and two A-levels. Many successful candidates are graduates or hold BTEC Higher National awards.

Clerical posts
☛ There are no longer any nationally applied educational requirements and recruitment is carried out locally. Some agencies will require five GCSEs at grades A, B or C including English and for posts as clerical assistants two GCSEs at grades A, B or C including English.

✍ **Further information** Recruitment and Assessment Services Agency, Alençon Link, Basingstoke, Hampshire RE21 1JB (Fast stream only)

▥ **Reading** *Working In* Series: *Working in the Civil Service* published by and available from the Careers and Occupational Information Centre, price £2.65

☛ School careers library classification CAB

Clerical
see **Civil Service, Local Government Administration** *and* **Secretarial Work**

Community Work
see **Youth and Community Work**

Company Secretaryship

A company secretary acts as a company's legal representative and ensures that it operates within the law. Company secretaries are responsible for keeping a register of shareholders and calling shareholders' meetings, paying dividends on shares and taking minutes at Board meetings. They may also advise the Board on financial and legal matters. In some companies the company secretary may also carry out personnel and other administrative functions.

☛ Three-year full-time or equivalent part-time course for the examinations of the Institute of Chartered Secretaries and Administrators (ICSA). The ICSA's Open Access policy means that anyone who is 17 years of age or over can study for the ICSA examinations on the Foundation Programme without previous academic qualifications.

☛ Entry after higher education: see Higher Education on page 132. Any degree will give exemption from the Foundation and the Pre-professional stages. BTEC Higher award holders will also gain exemptions.

Note: The Institute's examinations are designed for general administrators as well as company secretaries.

✍ **Further information** Institute of Chartered Secretaries and Administrators, 16 Park Crescent, London WIN 4AH

▥ **Reading** First Enquiry packs are available free from the Institute

☛ School careers library classification CAP

Computing Work and Information Technology

Although most people will find some aspects of their working life affected by computers, computing personnel specialise and work solely in computing and information technology.

Data entry, transferring information by typing from paper to a form that the computer can 'read', is normally part of clerical or secretarial work (see Secretarial work)

☞ On-the-job training or computer-familiarity courses at further education colleges. Some GCSEs not necessarily at grades A, B or C are generally required.

Computer programmers write the code for the instructions (program) to operate the computer. The equipment is known as hardware and the programming side software.

☞ Part-time, day-release or evening classes for the City and Guilds Certificate in Basic Computer Programming. GCSE mathematics is often required. Some employers stipulate 18 as a minimum age.

☞ Part-time, sandwich, block-release and full-time courses for the BTEC National Certificate/Diploma in computer studies. Four GCSEs at grades A, B or C or a BTEC First Certificate/Diploma are required.

Systems analysts understand and interpret the way a business organisation manages its work, including the use of its computers. They advise on and design the computer system.

Software engineers work in teams to design and update software (large scale programs) frequently constructed from existing 'library' programs.

☞ Two-year full-time or three-year sandwich courses for the BTEC Higher National Diploma in computing or in software engineering or in mathematics, statistics and computing. Three GCSEs at grades A, B or C including mathematics and one A-level or a BTEC National award is required for entry. Part-time courses leading to the BTEC Higher National Certificate in computer studies have the same entry requirements as the Higher National Diploma.

☛ Entry after higher education: see Higher Education on page 132. Formerly graduates of all degree subjects were recruited for computing but now most successful candidates have taken degree courses with some computer content. Degrees in computing require a good base of GCSEs including good grades in English and mathematics and at least two A-levels. Some colleges require A-level mathematics.

✍ **Further information** British Computer Society, PO Box 1454, Station Rd, Swindon SN1 1TG

National Computing Centre, Bracken House, Charles Street, Manchester M1 7BD

▥ **Reading** *Working In* Series: *Computing* published by and available from the Careers and Occupational Information Centre, price £2.35

Computer Science Degree Course Guide published by Hobsons Publishing PLC, price £5.95

☛ School careers library classification PAD

Consumer Advice Work
see Trading Standards Administration

Customs and Excise Work

Customs and excise officers are the civil servants who are responsible for the collection of customs duties and the prevention of the illegal import and export of prohibited goods such as drugs and firearms. This is only a small proportion of their work, for they are responsible for the collection of Value Added Tax (VAT) and Excise duties on oil, petrol, tobacco, wine and spirits.

Executive Officer
☛ Three GCSEs at grades A, B or C including English

and two A-levels are required. All subjects are acceptable. Minimum age $17^{1}/_{2}$. In practice many entrants are graduates or holders of BTEC Higher awards.

Administrative Officer
(formerly Clerical Officer)
☞ Five GCSEs at grades A, B or C including English are required. All subjects are acceptable. Local recruitment.

Administrative Assistant
(formerly Clerical Assistant)
Two GCSEs at grades A, B or C including English are required. Local recruitment.

✍ **Further information**
Recruitment and Assessment Services Agency, Alençon Link, Basingstoke, Hampshire RG21 1JB
Local Collector of Customs and Excise (address from the local telephone directory)

📖 **Reading** *Executive Opportunities in HM Customs and Excise* published by and available free from Personnel Division A2, HM Customs and Excise, 6th Floor Central, New King's Beam House, 22 Upper Ground, London SE1 9PJ
☞ School careers library classification CAB

Dairy Farming
see **Farming and Agricultural Advisory Work**

Dairy Technology

Dairy technologists apply their scientific training to the collection, storage and processing of milk and the manufacture of a wide range of milk-based products such as cheese, yogurts and ice-cream.
☞ Two-year full-time, three-year sandwich or part-time courses for the BTEC National Certificate/Diploma in

Science (technology of food) specialising in dairy technology. Four GCSEs at grades A, B or C including mathematics and science or a BTEC First Certificate/Diploma in Science is required. This can be followed by a BTEC Higher National Diploma in Science (technology of food). Alternative entry qualifications for the BTEC Higher National courses are one A-level in a science subject and GCSEs at grades A, B or C in English and a subject demonstrating numeracy.

☛ Entry after higher education: see Higher Education on page 132. Degrees in food science or technology require a good base of GCSEs at grades A, B or C including double award science followed by chemistry and two other science or mathematics subjects at A-level or a BTEC National Diploma in science.

✍ **Further information** Dairy Trade Federation, 19 Cornwall Terrace, London NW1 4QP

▥ **Reading** *Food for your future* and *The Dairy Industry Employment Directory* published by the National Dairy Council and available free from the Dairy Trade Federation

☛ School careers library classification SAB

Dancing

Dancers may work as stage performers of ballet, contemporary and modern dance, teach children and adults, or plan dance sequences which is known as choreography.

☛ For diploma courses GCSEs at grades A, B or C in English and mathematics are required. For degree courses two A-levels as well as a good base of GCSEs are required. For the courses leading to recognised teacher status the entrance requirements are the same as those of other teaching courses.

✍ **Further information** Council for Dance Education and Training (CDET), 5 Tavistock Place, London WC1H 9SS

||||| Reading CDET publishes a range of information leaflets covering various areas of dance training. These are available free if a large stamped addressed envelope is sent.
☞ School careers library classification GAF

Data Processing
see **Computing Work and Information Technology**

Decorating
see **Building Crafts** *and* **Art and Design**

Dental Hygiene Work

Dental hygienists work under the direction of a dentist. They scale, clean and polish teeth, apply preventive materials which help reduce dental decay and give oral hygiene instruction.

☞ Full-time course lasting about one year for the Diploma in Dental Hygiene. Five GCSEs at grades A, B or C including at least a single award science are required. All candidates should normally have had two years' experience as a dental surgery assistant and preferably hold a nationally recognised certificate in dental surgery assisting. Minimum age 17.

✍ **Further information** General Dental Council, 37 Wimpole Street, London W1M 8DQ
British Dental Hygienists Association, 64 Wimpole Street, London W1M 8AL

||||| Reading *Dental Hygienist* published by and available free from the General Dental Council
☞ School careers library classification JAF

Dental Surgery Assisting

Dental surgery assistants help the dentist by preparing materials and equipment, assisting at the chairside, sterilising instruments, looking after patients and doing paperwork.

☛ One- or two-year full-time, day-release or evening course at dental hospitals and colleges of further education. There are no longer any academic entry requirements, age limits or experience requirements to take the National Certificate for Dental Surgery Assistants.

✍ **Further information** The Association of British Dental Surgery Assistants, 29 London Street, Fleetwood, Lancashire FY7 6JY

▥ **Reading** *Dental Surgery Assisting as a Career* published by and available free from the Association
Dental Surgery Assistant published by and available free from the General Dental Council

☛ School careers library classification JAF

Dental Technician Work

Dental technicians construct and repair false teeth, crowns, and the orthodontic appliances which are used for straightening teeth. Their work is initiated by a prescription from a dentist.

☛ Three-year full-time, four-year sandwich or five-year day-release course while working in a laboratory for the BTEC National Diploma in Science (Dental Technology). Four GCSEs at grades A, B or C including mathematics and preferably double award science or a BTEC First Certificate are required for entry.

✍ **Further information** The Training Officer, The Dental Laboratories Association, Chapel House, Noel Street, Nottingham NG7 6AS
Dental Technicians Standards and Training Advisory Board, 64 Wimpole Street, London W1M 8DQ

▥ **Reading** *The Dental Technician* published by and available from A E Morgan Publications Ltd, Stanley House, 9 West Street, Epsom, Surrey KT18 7RL

The Dental Technician published by and available free from the Dental Technicians Standards and Training Advisory Board

☛ School careers library classification JAF

Dental Therapy Work

Dental therapists, who used to be called dental auxiliaries, work under the direction of a dentist in a hospital, community dental service or school dental clinic. They do simple fillings, extract milk teeth and scale and polish teeth. They do not work for dentists in private practice.

☛ Two-year full-time course at the London Hospital which also includes qualification as a dental hygienist. Five GCSEs at grades A, B or C are required, preferably including English and at least a single award science as well as experience as a dental surgery assistant and the National Certificate for Dental Surgery Assistants. Minimum age 18. Only eight places are available each year.

✍ **Further information** Dental Auxiliary School, London Hospital Medical College, 36 New Road, London E1 2AX

▥ **Reading** *Dental Therapist* published by and available free from the General Dental Council, 37 Wimpole Street, London W1M 8DQ

☛ School careers library classification JAF

Dentistry

Dentists conserve teeth by filling, crowning and bridge-work and try to prevent dental disease. They take out teeth and design false teeth to replace them. They correct irregular teeth in children by using plates and braces: this is called orthodontics.

☛ A degree in dentistry is essential and entry to a degree course requires a good base of GCSEs at grades A, B or C together with three A-levels, one of which generally has to be chemistry with two others chosen from mathematics, physics and biological subjects. GCSEs at grades A, B or C in mathematics and double award science are recommended. Some longer courses are run for candidates who have arts or a mixture of arts and science A-levels. See Higher Education on page 132.

✍ **Further information** General Dental Council, 37 Wimpole Street, London W1M 8DQ

▥ **Reading** *Dentistry Degree Course Guide*, published by Hobsons Publishing PLC, price £5.95

☛ School careers library classification JAF

Design
see **Art and Design**

Dietetics

Dietitians are trained specialists who apply the science of nutrition to every day eating, by promoting good food habits in people of all ages. Many work in hospitals where they teach and advise patients on diet for certain diseases; others work in the community advising the elderly or schoolchildren.

☛ Four-year degree course in nutrition (with State Registration in dietetics) or a four-year degree course in dietetics. These courses usually require a good base of GCSEs at grades A, B or C including English and preferably double award science and mathematics. At least two A-levels in science preferably including chemistry are also required. Graduates who have studied human biochemistry and physiology to a suitable standard can take a two-year postgraduate diploma course. See Higher Education on page 132.

✍ **Further information** British Dietetic Association, 7th Floor, Elizabeth House, 22 Suffolk Street, Queensway, Birmingham B1 1LS

▥ **Reading** *How to qualify as a dietitian* published by

and available free from the British Dietetic Association; please enclose a large stamped addressed envelope
☞ School careers library classification JAV

Diplomatic Service
see **Civil Service**

Dispensing Assistant/Pharmacy Technician Work

Dispensing assistants help pharmacists to make up prescriptions; they work in hospitals and in chemists' shops.

☞ Two-year part-time (day-release or evening) course for the Society of Apothecaries' Pharmacy Technician's Certificate. Three academic GCSEs at grades A, B or C preferably including at least a single award in science are required. Minimum age for taking the examination 18. There is discussion about the future of the Certificate with the introduction of National Vocational Qualifications. Latest information can be gained from the Society.

☞ Three-year part-time course for the BTEC National Certificate in Science (Pharmaceutical). Four GCSEs at grades A, B or C including mathematics and single award science or a BTEC First Certificate/Diploma is required for entry.

✍ **Further information** The Society of Apothecaries of London, Black Friars Lane, London EC4V 6EJ
☞ School careers library classification JAG

Dispensing Optics

Dispensing opticians supply and fit glasses prescribed by a specially qualified doctor or an optometrist (ophthalmic optician). They do not test sight.

204   Part 2: The Careers Guide

☛ Part-time (day-release) courses at colleges of further education or by correspondence course, for the examinations of the Association of British Dispensing Opticians together with three years' employment. Five GCSEs at grades A, B or C including English or English literature and mathematics are required. All subjects are acceptable.

☛ Two-year full-time course for the examination of the Association of British Dispensing Opticians plus a year's experience following the final examination. Five GCSEs at grades A, B or C including English or English literature, either mathematics or at least a single award science are required. All subjects are acceptable.

✍ **Further information** Association of British Dispensing Opticians, 7 Hurlingham Business Park, Sullivan Road, London sw6 3DU

▥ **Reading** *A Career in Vision Care* published by and available free from the General Optical Council, 41 Harley Street, London w1N 2DJ

☛ School careers library classification JAL

Display Work
see **Art and Design**

Drama

Apart from acting which is a very overcrowded profession there are careers in stage production and stage management.

☛ Three-year full-time course in acting or stage management at a drama school. Academic qualifications are not as important as evidence of potential dramatic ability, although many drama students will have GCSEs and A-levels.

☛ Degree courses where drama is often combined with another subject. A good base of GCSEs at grades A, B or C is required with at least two A-levels. English is sometimes required at A-level. These are academic and are not stage training. Some colleges of higher education offer drama as part of a BEd course.

/// **Reading** Working In Series: *Performing Arts* published by and available from the Careers and Occupational Information Centre, price £2.35

☛ School careers library classification GAB

Dyeing

Dyeing is concerned with the production of coloured textile materials.

☛ Full-time or part-time college courses for a BTEC National Certificate/Diploma in Science (Textile Coloration). Four GCSEs at grades A, B or C including mathematics and at least single award science or a BTEC First Certificate/Diploma is required for entry. Successful students may subsequently take the BTEC Higher National Certificate/Diploma in Science (Textile Coloration) after a further two years. The Higher National courses can also be entered by candidates with three GCSEs including mathematics, single award science and a subject testing command of English and one A-level. Professional qualifications awarded by the Society of Dyers and Colourists – namely the Certificate in Coloration and the Associateship of the Society may be taken after a further one year and two years respectively.

☛ Entry after higher education: see Higher Education on page 132. Several universities run degree courses in colour chemistry. A good base of GCSEs at grades A, B or C is required and A-levels preferably in chemistry, mathematics and physics. Some chemistry students are able to take either special papers in colour chemistry or a postgraduate course in colour chemistry after completing their degree course.

✍ **Further information** The Society of Dyers and Colourists, Perkin House, PO Box 244, 82 Grattan Road, Bradford BD1 2JB

⑪ **Reading** *Careers in Colour* published by and available free from the Society of Dyers and Colourists
☞ School careers library classification QOB

Economics

Economists are social scientists who are concerned with questions such as the reasons for high unemployment, the balance of payments, the amount of public expenditure and the effect of taxation.

☞ A degree course is essential. A good base of GCSEs at grades A, B or C including mathematics and at least two A-levels are required. The A-levels may be in any subjects, although mathematics is often preferred. A-level economics is never required to enter a degree course. See Higher Education on page 132.

⑪ **Reading** *Economics Degree Course Guide* published by Hobsons Publishing PLC, price £5.95
☞ School careers library classification PAF

Electrical Engineering
see **Engineering**

Electronic and Radio Engineering
see **Engineering**

Engineering

Engineering covers an extremely wide field of careers. This section deals with the work of chartered engineers, incorporated engineers and engineering technicians. The next section deals with engineering craft work.

Aeronautical Engineering
The aircraft industry can be split into 'airframes' and

engines. Designing airframes includes aerodynamics, structural design and the design of the systems within the aircraft. Aerodynamics covers the basic shape of the aircraft related to performance. Structural design has become more complex because of the introduction of new materials. 'Systems' covers the heating and ventilation systems within the aircraft, the radar and the flight control. The 'engines' side of the industry requires aeronautical engineers particularly for the study of air flows inside the engines; many mechanical engineers also work on this side. In addition to doing design work, aeronautical engineers service and repair aircraft for airline operators and are employed by British Aerospace to develop and construct their communications and other satellites.

✍ **Further information** Royal Aeronautical Society, 4 Hamilton Place, London W1V 0BQ

☞ School careers library classification RAB

Chemical and Biochemical Engineering

Chemical engineering theory can be applied to a wide range of process industries because the processes can be split up into operations which are essentially the same. Thus distillation occurs in whisky manufacture and oil refining and filtration is common to sewage treatment, drugs manufacture and the concentration of mineral ores. Chemical engineers study these processes and design, construct and operate the plant in which they take place. Computer control and design is a standard feature of chemical engineering and all courses include training in this field. Safety and environmental issues are high on the agenda of chemical engineers who can make a positive contribution in the design and running of plants.

✍ **Further information** The Institution of Chemical Engineers, 12 Gayfere Street, London SW1P 3HP

☞ School careers library classification RAG

Civil Engineering

Civil engineers plan, design, construct and maintain

roads, railways, airports, bridges, tunnels, water supplies and reservoirs. The supply and distribution of energy is also an area of work for civil engineers who design and build North Sea oil platforms, pipelines and hydro-electric schemes.

Structural engineering is a specialised area of civil engineering. It is the science and art of designing and constructing structures such as bridges, the framework and foundations of large buildings, oil rigs, aircraft and space structures.

Many civil engineers work for local authorities where they are in charge of the building of roads and bridges and also concerned with street lighting, refuse collection and the control of pollution. Transportation planning which deals with traffic management schemes such as one-way streets and siting of roundabouts, traffic lights and car parks as well as the effective operation of public transport overlaps with town and country planning. Civil engineers help developing countries with irrigation schemes, sanitation and transport which are essential to combat disease and malnutrition.

✍ **Further information** Civil Engineering Careers Service, 1–7 Great George Street, London SW1P 3AA Institution of Structural Engineers, 11 Upper Belgrave Street, London SW1X 8BH

☛ School careers library classification UN

Electrical and Electronic Engineering

Electrical engineers are responsible for generating electricity and then bringing it to heat and light buildings and to provide a continuous source of power for equipment used in homes, schools, offices and hospitals. It is the electrical engineers who will work out new methods of producing electricity when our traditional resources no longer exist.

Electronic engineers work in the rapidly expanding field of communications. Microelectronic technology has enabled these engineers to develop highly sophisticated computers and information systems which are now being used in transport, business, industry and medicine. Computers control industrial processes and robots are now widely used in industrial production. Particularly important are the life-saving applications of micro-electronics in hospitals: heart-lung machines and kidney dialysers, etc.

✍ **Further information** Schools Education & Liaison Service, Institution of Electrical Engineers, Michael Faraday House, Six Hills Way, Stevenage, Hertfordshire SG1 2AY

☛ School careers library classification RAK and RAL

Energy Engineering

Energy engineers apply their scientific knowledge to the preparation and burning of coal, gas, oil and nuclear fuel for heating, lighting and power. Some may work in fuel conservation, being concerned with the most efficient use of the earth's dwindling supplies of fossil fuels.

Gas engineers mainly work for British Gas supplying gas to consumers in Great Britain. They also work for companies making gas appliances such as cookers, fires and boilers. Gas engineering covers both civil engineering – the provision of pipelines and gas holders – and chemical engineering, producing gas from coal or oil and the exploration for further gas supplies. Since the discovery and use of natural gas in the UK, the gas industry has expanded and there are more opportunities for gas engineers.

✍ **Further information** Institute of Energy, 18 Devonshire Street, London W1N 2AU

The Institution of Gas Engineers, 17 Grosvenor Crescent, London SW1X 7ES

☛ School careers library classification RAN

Maritime Engineering

Marine engineers work on the design, construction,

operation and maintenance of ships' engines and systems. Many work in the Merchant Navy as engineer officers where they are responsible for the safe and efficient operation of the ship's engines and associated systems. **Naval architects** are not concerned with the engines that move the ship through the water, but with the design, construction, stability and performance of the ship's hull and various types of construction in the offshore industry.

Marine engineers and naval architects work in close co-operation on projects in offshore/subsea engineering, structural, mechanical, civil and electrical engineering with marine applications.

✍ **Further information** Institute of Marine Engineers, The Memorial Building, 76 Mark Lane, London EC3R 7JN Royal Institution of Naval Architects, 10 Upper Belgrave Street, London SW1X 8BQ

☛ School careers library classification RAV and ROF

Mechanical Engineering

Mechanical engineering includes most technical activities in which moving parts are involved. Mechanical engineers work closely with engineers of other disciplines and work in design, manufacture, installation, operation and maintenance of machinery of all kinds. They work in fields as diverse as bio-mechanics, satellite systems, nuclear power, materials science and food technologies.

✍ **Further information** Schools Liaison Service, Institution of Mechanical Engineers, Northgate Avenue, Bury St Edmunds, Suffolk IP32 6BN

☛ School careers library classification RAX

Mining Engineering

Mining engineers design and manage mining operations so they are profitable, safe and harm the environment as little as possible. There are specialist opportunities in ventilation, environmental engineering, rock mechanics, prospecting, mineral processing, mining surveying and drilling engineering. Most openings in the UK are with British Coal and a growing number of quarrying companies but there are many opportunities abroad in metal mining.

✍ **Further information** Institution of Mining Engineers, Danum House, South Parade, Doncaster DN1 2DY

Institution of Mining and Metallurgy, 44 Portland Place, London WIN 4BR

☛ School careers library classification ROB

Education and Training

Chartered Engineer (CEng) If you are planning from the outset to be a chartered engineer you should have a good base of GCSEs at grades A, B or C including mathematics, double award science and preferably English for later specialisation in sciences at A-level. Most accredited degree courses leading to chartered engineer status require A-levels in mathematics and physics; for courses in chemical engineering A-levels in mathematics and chemistry are generally required. A good BTEC National Certificate/Diploma is an alternative entry qualification. You should take a full-time or sandwich degree course in engineering at a university or college of higher education that has been accredited by a professional engineering institution. Such a course exempts students from the examinations of the Engineering Council. Some engineering companies sponsor students on these courses.

In addition to the courses you must undergo a two-year period of practical training and two years of professional responsibility. This will vary according to the institution you join but will not be less than four years in total. To be registered as a chartered engineer you must also have corporate membership of one of the institutions of the Chartered Engineer Section of the Board for Engineers Registration of the Engineering Council.

Incorporated Engineer (IEng) Two-year full-time or three-year sandwich or equivalent part-time accredited courses for the BTEC Higher National Diploma/ Certificate in engineering for which the entry requirements are four GCSEs at grades A, B or C and two subjects, usually mathematics and physics, will have been studied to A-level and one of these passed at A-level. The most useful GCSE subjects would be English, mathematics, computer studies, technology and double award science. A BTEC National Certificate/Diploma with relevant units is an alternative entry qualification to BTEC higher award courses. In addition to an academic course, for IEng you must have four years' relevant engineering experience including two years' approved practical training. To be registered as an incorporated engineer you must also have membership of one of the institutions of the Incorporated Engineer Section of the Board for Engineers Registration of the Engineering Council.

Engineering Technician (EngTech) For entry to a two- or three-year BTEC National Certificate/Diploma programme four GCSEs at grades A, B or C or a BTEC First Certificate/Diploma in Engineering is required. In addition you must have three years' engineering experience including two years' approved practical training and are encouraged to become a member of one of the institutions of the engineering technician section of the Board of Engineers Registration of the Engineering Council.

Engineering Council: Board for Engineers Registration

The Engineering Council, a Royal Chartered body set up in 1981 to promote the science and practice of engineering, has taken over the principal responsibility for the registration of engineers in collaboration with the individual professional institutions. The following are constituent members of the Board for Engineers Registration. It is important to note that a member institution may require qualifications that differ from, or are additional to, those called for by the Board and this should be checked with the particular institution concerned.

1 Chartered engineer entry
2 Incorporated engineer entry
3 Engineering technician entry

Association of Cost Engineers 1
Biological Engineering Society 1 (Affiliate) 2, 3
British Computer Society 1, 2
British Institute of Non-Destructive Testing 1
    (Affiliate) 2, 3
Chartered Institution of Building Services Engineers 1, 2, 3
Institute of Acoustics 1 (Affiliate) 2
Institute of British Foundrymen 1 (Affiliate) 2, 3
Institute of Energy 1, 2
Institute of Engineers and Technicians 2, 3
Institute of Highway Incorporated Engineers 2, 3
Institute of Hospital Engineering 1 (Affiliate) 2, 3
Institute of Marine Engineers 1, 2, 3
Institute of Measurement and Control 1, 2, 3
Institute of Materials 1, 2, 3
Institute of Physics 1 (Affiliate)
Institute of Plumbing 2, 3
Institute of Quality Assurance 2, 3
Institute of Road Transport Engineers 2, 3
Institution of Agricultural Engineers 1 (Affiliate) 2, 3
Institution of Chemical Engineers 1, 2
Institution of Civil Engineers 1, 2, 3
Institution of Electrical Engineers 1
Institution of Electronics and Electrical Incorporated
    Engineers 2, 3
Institution of Engineering Designers 1 (Affiliate) 2, 3
Institution of Gas Engineers 1, 2, 3

Institution of Incorporated Executive Engineers 2, 3
Institution of Lighting Engineers 1 (Affiliate) 2, 3
Institution of Mechanical Engineers 1
Institution of Mechanical and Incorporated Engineers 2, 3
Institution of Mining Electrical and Mining Mechanical
   Engineers 1 (Affiliate) 2, 3
Institution of Mining Engineers 1, 2, 3
Institution of Mining and Metallurgy 1, 2
Institution of Nuclear Engineers 1 (Affiliate) 2
Institution of Plant Engineers 1 (Affiliate) 2, 3
Institution of Structural Engineers 1, 2
Institution of Water and Environmental Management 1
   (Affiliate) 2, 3
Institution of Water Officers 2, 3
Institution of Works and Highways Management 2, 3
Minerals Engineering Society 1 (Affiliate) 2, 3
North East Coast Institution of Engineers and
   Shipbuilders 1 (Affiliate) 2, 3
Royal Aeronautical Society 1, 2, 3
Royal Institution of Naval Architects 1, 2, 3
Welding Institute 1 (Affiliate) 2, 3

✍ **Further information** Engineering Council,
10 Maltravers Street, London WC2R 3ER
Engineering Training Authority, Careers and Information
Services, Vector House, 41 Clarendon Road, Watford,
Hertfordshire WD1 1HS (for careers in manufacturing
industry)
Civil Engineering Careers Service, 1–7 Great George
Street, London SW1P 3AA
Women's Engineering Society, Department of Civil
Engineering, Imperial College of Science and Technology,
Imperial College Road, London SW7 2BU
Individual institutions

📶 **Reading** A range of free leaflets is published by and
available from the Engineering Training Authority and
the Civil Engineering Careers Service. Please specify the
level of career that interests you.

☞ School careers library classification R

Engineering Crafts

Engineering craftsmen and women are skilled workers able to follow engineering drawings and instructions prepared by professional engineers. In manufacturing industry, where the majority of engineering craftspeople work, they can be divided into

(i) craft machinists who shape metal into components. Turners use lathes which rotate a workpiece from which metal is removed with a fixed cutting tool. Millers use milling machines which remove metal from a fixed workpiece. Toolmakers make a variety of tools such as jigs, fixtures and cutters which are used in the production process.

(ii) fitters and electricians: fitters assemble machines in factories deciding on the order of the work needed to make sure the parts fit and work together. They also repair and maintain machines on the customers' premises – in factories as well as private houses. So a gas fitter, for example, will repair gas stoves, gas fires and central heating boilers, finding faults and correcting them. Electricians work on electrical installation, putting electrical systems into new buildings or replacing them in old buildings. They repair electrical equipment, including both ordinary household appliances and industrial machinery. Electronics servicing covers the repair of radio, TV and of other electronic equipment such as computers.

(iii) metal fabrication workers. Welders join or cut metal using oxy-acetylene or other types of equipment. Sheet metal workers make complicated shaped items from thin metal sheets.

(iv) metal processors. A moulder reproduces the shape of a component in reverse form in a sand mould. Molten metal is poured into the completed mould to form a casting.

☛ Three–four year apprenticeship with a firm. The majority of craft trainees follow the training pattern recommended by the Engineering Training Authority (ENTRA). The first year is spent at training centres approved by ENTRA, the second and third years are spent in 'module training' either within the firm or at a centre which has specialist facilities. Trainees can in addition take City and Guilds or BTEC courses at local further education colleges. Some firms offer Youth Training Scheme (YT) courses. There are no formal entry requirements but most employers give preference to candidates with GCSEs at around grade E or higher in mathematics, science, computer studies and technological subjects.

An important engineering craft level career outside manufacturing industry is the motor mechanic who repairs all types of road vehicles. They usually specialise in light vehicles such as cars and vans, or in heavy vehicles, eg lorries and buses or motorbikes. In most garages mechanics either do repairs and servicing or do bodywork which can include panel beating, welding and spray painting.

☛ Day-release, block-release or evening courses at colleges of further education for City and Guilds certificates while working in a garage. There are no formal entry qualifications but employers may give preference to candidates with GCSEs at around grade E or higher in mathematics, science and technological subjects.

✍ **Further information** Engineering Training Authority, Careers and Information Service, Vector House, 41 Clarendon Road, Watford, Hertfordshire WD1 1HS (for careers in manufacturing industry)

▥ **Reading** Booklets published by and available free from the Engineering Training Authority Careers and Information Service

☛ School careers library classification: various under R

Environmental Health

Environmental health officers work for local authorities to ensure a healthy environment for us all. They inspect housing, restaurants and shops where food is sold. They monitor levels of air pollution and deal with complaints about excessive noise. There are increasing opportunities in the private sector.

☛ Four-year sandwich course leading to a degree in environmental health. Three GCSEs at grades A, B or C including mathematics, English and at least a single award science and two A-levels, one of which must be a science subject, are normally required. Some part-time degree courses are available. See Higher Education on page 132.

✍ **Further information** Institution of Environmental Health Officers, Chadwick House, Rushworth Street, London SE1 0QT

▥ **Reading** *EHO: The Role of the Environmental Health Officer* and *A Career in Environmental Health* both available free from the Institution

☛ School careers library classification COP

Estate Agency, Auctioneering and Valuation

Estate agents act for people wishing to sell property – not only houses but also farms, factories, shops and offices. They arrange mortgages and also manage property on behalf of landlords – collecting rents and arranging for repairs to be done. Auctioneers sell property as well as animals, furniture and second-hand goods. Valuers assess the value of all types of property for rates, tax, probate and insurance purposes. They work in local authorities, the Inland Revenue and for estate agents and auctioneers. Estate agents and auctioneers do not have to be professionally qualified but many have one of the following qualifications.

☛ Part-time study for the examinations of the Architects and Surveyors Institute using the syllabus of the Confederation of Construction Professions; details from the Institute.

☛ Three-year full-time course, or an equivalent part-time or correspondence course for the examinations of the Incorporated Society of Valuers and Auctioneers. Five GCSEs at grades A, B or C including English and mathematics, or four GCSEs at grades A, B or C and one A-level including English and mathematics at either level is required for entry.

☛ Three- to four-year part-time course for the examinations of the Institute of Revenues, Rating and Valuation. Two A-levels and two GCSEs at grades A, B or C or one A-level and four GCSEs at grades A, B or C including English and mathematics are required. All GCSE and A-level subjects are acceptable.

☛ Part-time study for the examinations of the Incorporated Association of Architects and Surveyors. Three GCSEs at grades A, B or C and two A-levels are required. Mathematics, science and a subject requiring the use of descriptive English must be included at either level.

☛ Three-year full-time or four-year sandwich course for a recognised degree in estate management or building surveying. Three GCSEs at grades A, B or C and two A-levels are required. English and mathematics must be passed at either level. These degree courses give various exemptions from the examinations of the professional bodies: details from the individual professional bodies.

☛ Full-time or part-time college courses for a BTEC National Certificate/Diploma in Land Use (Estate Management). Four GCSEs at grades A, B or C preferably including English and mathematics or a BTEC First Certificate/Diploma are required for entry. A BTEC National course can be followed by a degree course (above), professional qualifications or a BTEC Higher

National Certificate/Diploma in Estate Management.
Alternative entry requirements to HND are four GCSEs at
grades A, B or C including English and mathematics and
one A-level.

✐ **Further information** Incorporated Association of
Architects and Surveyors, Jubilee House, Billing Brook
Road, Weston Favell, Northampton NN3 1TU
Incorporated Society of Valuers and Auctioneers,
3 Cadogan Gate, London SW1X 0AS
Institute of Revenues, Rating and Valuation, 41 Doughty
Street, London WC1N 2LF
Architects and Surveyors Institute, 15 St Mary Street,
Chippenham, Wiltshire SN15 3JN
The Royal Institution of Chartered Surveyors, Surveyor
Court, Westwood Way, Coventry CV4 8JE

▥ **Reading** *Making Land, Property and Construction
Work* published by and available free from the Royal
Institution of Chartered Surveyors
Booklets published by and available free from the
Incorporated Society of Valuers and Auctioneers

☛ School careers library classification UM

Exporting

Exporters work in the marketing departments of large
companies, in import/export agencies and in confirming
houses. They obtain orders from overseas for British goods,
undertake the necessary documentation and arrange for
the goods to be shipped or air freighted. Some large
British companies maintain subsidiary companies abroad.

☛ Part-time study for the examinations of the Institute
of Export. Four GCSEs at grades A, B or C are required
including English. Many employers prefer mathematics,
geography and a modern foreign language at GCSE. The
following subjects are not acceptable: art, child
development, drama and music. For those with no
academic qualifications the Institute of Export's

Certificate in Export Office Practice is available at some colleges. Minimum age 18.

☛ One-year day-release or evening course for the Advanced Certificate in Overseas Trade/Professional Examination Part I. Four GCSEs at grades A, B or C including English and one A-level is required. Minimum age 18. This course is also accepted as part of the qualification of the Institute of Freight Forwarders. The Chartered Institute of Marketing may give exemptions from their Certificate and Diploma examinations to successful candidates. Students can follow this with study for the Professional Part II/Diploma in Export Management.

☛ Two-year full-time or sandwich or three-year part-time course for the BTEC Higher National Diploma. At some colleges it is possible to take options in marketing. Three GCSEs at grades A, B or C and one A-level or a BTEC National Certificate or Diploma are required for entry.

☛ Three-year full-time or four-year sandwich course for a degree in business studies. Three GCSEs at grades A, B or C (many colleges require English and mathematics) and two A-levels are required. Some courses have options in international marketing. It is also possible at some universities to take degree courses in international marketing, usually as part of a modular programme. See Higher Education on page 132 about entry to higher education. Postgraduate courses in exporting are also available.

✍ **Further information** Institute of Export, 64 Clifton Street, London EC2A 4HB

▥ **Reading** *As a Professional Exporter* published by and available free from the Institute of Export

☛ School careers library classification OS

Farming and Agricultural Advisory Work

Farming covers a wide variety of work and offers jobs for people at all levels of educational attainment. There are mixed farms – those with crops and livestock – but over the last few years there has been a tendency for farms to specialise in dairy cows, beef cattle, pigs, sheep, poultry or cereals. For agricultural advisory work or research a degree is usually required. Growing vegetables and fruit in market gardens is dealt with under Horticulture. All the courses below degree level will be replaced by National Vocational Qualifications (NVQ) over the next few years. Degree courses will eventually be linked with the NVQ system.

☛ Most 16 and 17 year-old school-leavers enter the industry through Youth Training (YT) schemes which are most commonly managed by local agricultural colleges and departments. The one-or two-year schemes offer planned work experience on farms and vocational education and training through day and block release courses which will, in the future, lead to National Vocational Qualifications (NVQ) at Levels 1 and 2. There are no specific educational requirements but preference may be given to candidates who have some GCSEs at grades E and above.

☛ One-year full-time course for the National Certificate in general agriculture, dairy farming or poultry husbandry. No formal entry qualifications are necessary but GCSEs at grade E or above in English, mathematics and at least a single award science would be helpful. At least one year's practical experience is essential. Students who achieve a high standard in the National Certificate can follow it with a one-year supplementary course for either the Advanced National Certificate in Agriculture or the National Certificate in Farm Management.

☛ Three-year sandwich course for the BTEC National Diploma in Agriculture. The second year is spent working on a farm. Four GCSEs at grades A, B or C including double award science and one testing command of English are required. On the course students can specialise in arable farming, livestock production, farm mechanisation or dairy farming. There is a separate two-year sandwich course in poultry husbandry. It is also possible to enter these courses with a good National Certificate.

☛ Three-year sandwich course for the BTEC Higher National Diploma in Agriculture. Four GCSEs including a subject testing command of English and two distinct mathematics/science subjects and one A-level normally in a science subject and another subject studied to A-level are required. Candidates may also enter with BTEC National Diplomas in science or agriculture.

☛ Three-year degree course in agriculture for which a good base of GCSEs at grades A, B or C including mathematics and double award science for later specialisation in A-level science subjects is required. See Higher Education on page 132 about entry to higher education.

✍ **Further information** Careers, Education and Training for Agriculture and the Countryside, 10 Northgate Street, Warwick CV34 4SR
National Examinations Board for Agriculture, Horticulture and Allied Industries, 46 Britannia Street, London WC1X 9RG
Business and Technology Education Council, Central House, Upper Woburn Place, London WC1H 0HH

📖 **Reading** *Agricultural Sciences Degree Course Guide* published for CRAC by Hobsons Publishing PLC, price £5.95
Directory of Courses in Land Based Industries published annually by East Anglian Regional Advisory Council for

Further Education, 2 Looms Lane, Bury St Edmunds,
Suffolk IP33 1HE. Telephone them on 0284 764977 for
availability and cost.

Factsheets on courses in agriculture and related
subjects published by and available free from the Business
and Technology Education Council
Working In Series: *Agriculture and Horticulture* published
by and available from the Careers and Occupational
Information Centre price £2.35
☛ School careers library classification WAB

Fashion – Clothing Production

Most clothes are mass produced in factories. A team of
skilled clothing-production workers use mass-production
techniques to translate the design into a finished garment.

Cutters use an electric knife (sometimes computerised
cutting machinery) to cut out the separate pieces which
make up each garment. Sewing machinists put the
garment together often using a specialised machine for
each process. Pressers use a mechanical press or a hand
iron on the garments at stages in the production process
and when the garment has been completed. Examiners
inspect the garments at various stages to make sure faults
are spotted and repaired. There are also management and
technician level posts concerned with engineering, design
(see Art and design), production planning, and financial
planning and control.
☛ For cutters, sewing machinists, pressers and
examiners: on-the-job training sometimes with day
release to attend courses at colleges of further education.
Many of these courses lead to City and Guilds Certificates.
No formal educational qualifications are required but some
employers give preference to candidates with GCSEs at grade
E or above. Many school leavers now enter the
industry through Youth Training (YT). National Council for

Vocational Qualifications (NCVQ) certificates are being introduced at Levels 1 and 2 covering various skills and competencies.

Management and Technician Careers

☛ Two-year full-time course for the BTEC Higher National Diploma in Clothing for which either four GCSEs at grades A, B or C and one A-level or a BTEC National Diploma in Clothing is required.

☛ Four-year sandwich course for the examinations of the Clothing and Footwear Institute (CFI International). Five GCSEs at grades A, B or C including English and either mathematics or science and one A-level are required. All GCSE and A-level subjects are acceptable. After successful completion of the examinations and two years' experience in the clothing industry candidates qualify for the associateship of the Clothing and Footwear Institute (CFI International) which is degree equivalent.

☛ Four-year sandwich course leading to a degree in clothing studies. A good base of GCSEs at grades A, B or C including English and mathematics and two A-levels are required. See Higher Education on page 132 about entry to higher education.

✍ **Further information** Clothing and Footwear Institute (CFI International), Butlers Wharf Business Centre, Suite 105, 45 Curlew Street, London SE1 2ND
Careers Information Service, Clothing and Allied Products Industrial Training Board (CAPITB plc), 80 Richardshaw Lane, Pudsey, Leeds LS28 6BN

▥ **Reading** *Working In* series: *Fashion* published by and available from the Careers and Occupational Information Centre, price £2.65

☛ School careers library classification EJ/SAH

Film and Video Production

Films and videos are made by a team composed of a camera operator, a sound recordist and a lighting specialist. A film editor then takes the film and cuts down the amount of footage shot. The director supervises the whole process. Depending on the size of the production the team may be composed of two or three people or over thirty. Animated films (cartoons) are also produced by a team who, in addition to the work of an ordinary film, draw all the pictures. The British film industry is very small and outside the television companies there are few opportunities. For entry to all courses it is important to show an amateur interest in film and video making.

☛ Three-year full-time course for a degree in art and design specialising in film production. A minimum of five GCSEs at grades A, B or C and either two A-levels or the completion of a foundation course in art and design is required.

☛ Three-year full-time course for a degree in film and photography. A good base of GCSEs at grades A, B or C including English and science, and at least two A-levels are required.

☛ A range of other courses is available. Entry qualifications vary from a good general education to a degree or comparable qualification.

☛ On-the-job training lasting about a year for BBC camera operators, sound operators, or assistant film editors. Candidates should be at least GCSE grades A, B or C standard in a range of subjects and have an informed knowledge of the principles of cinematography and a lively interest in films and film-making. There are many candidates for every vacancy, so in practice much higher qualifications are required. Successful candidates usually have degrees or experience in film-making.

✍ **Further information** British Film Institute, 21 Stephen Street, London w1p 1pl

▥ **Reading** *Film and Television Training* published by and available from the Institute, price £4.25 including postage
Studying Film and Television published by and available from the Institute, price £4.25 including postage (when both books ordered together, £7.00 including postage)
☛ School careers library classification GAL

Fine Art
see **Art and Design**

Fire-Fighting

Fire-fighters not only fight fires and save lives, they deal with all types of emergencies such as road accidents and spillage of dangerous chemicals. They also inspect buildings to make sure that they comply with the fire-prevention rules and instruct members of the public in fire-fighting techniques.

☛ Most brigades do not have formal entry qualifications but candidates with GCSEs at grade E or above in English, mathematics and double award science are most likely to satisfactorily complete the entrance tests. These consist of a series of ability range tests, assembled at national level, specifically for potential recruits to the fire service, together with interviews and, in some brigades, numeracy and literacy tests. Candidates must have good eyesight and pass a vigorous medical examination as fire-fighters have to be physically fit and agile. The minimum age is 18, although some brigades have a junior recruitment scheme with entry at 16. All candidates who are selected must successfully complete a 12-week basic course which is usually residential. Promotion is from within the service and only for those members who have passed the written and practical examinations.

✍ **Further information** Fire brigade headquarters (the address will be in the local telephone directory)

▥ Reading *And We Also Fight Fires – A Career in the Fire Service* published by and available free from the Home Office (Fire Department), Queen Anne's Gate, London SW1H 9AT and local fire brigade headquarters
Working In Series: *The Emergency Services* published by and available from the Careers and Occupational Information Centre, price £2.50
☛ School careers library classification MAF

Floristry
see **Retail and Wholesale Distribution**

Food Science and Technology

Food scientists examine the chemistry and biology of foods from raw materials through processing to the final product. Food technologists use food science and other technological know-how to turn raw materials into finished products for the consumer.

☛ Two-year full-time or three-year sandwich course for the BTEC National Certificate/Diploma in Science (Technology of Food). Normally four GCSEs at grades A, B or C including double award science and preferably English or a BTEC First Certificate/Diploma are required for entry.

☛ Two-year full-time or three-year sandwich courses for the BTEC Higher National Diploma in Science (Technology of Food). One A-level in a science subject, GCSEs at grades A, B or C in English and a subject demonstrating numeracy or a BTEC National Certificate or Diploma in the technology of food or in science with appropriate units is required.

☛ A good base of GCSEs at grades A, B or C and at least two science A-levels are required for a degree in food science and technology. Chemistry A-level is normally essential. Graduates with science degrees can take postgraduate courses in food science. See Higher Education on page 132.

✍ **Further information** Institute of Food Science and Technology, 5 Cambridge Court, 210 Shepherd's Bush Road, London w6 7NL

Food Manufacturers' Council for Industrial Training, 6 Catherine Street, London wcsb 5JJ

📖 **Reading** *Careers in Food Science and Technology* and *Where to Study for a Career in Food Science and Technology* published by and single copies available free from the Institute. Please enclose an 8¹/₂" x 6¹/₂" stamped addressed envelope

☞ School careers library classification QON/SAB

Forestry

Forestry work is concerned with managing forests and includes planting, tending, felling and the preparation and marketing of timber. About half the people in forestry work are employed by the Forestry Commission; the remainder work for commercial forestry farms, large forest estates and local authorities.

☞ Most 16 and 17 year-old school-leavers enter the industry through Youth Training (YT) which is either managed by local agricultural colleges or other approved training organisations. The one-and two-year schemes offer planned work experience and education through day and block release courses leading to National Vocational qualifications at Levels 1 and 2. This training leads to posts as forest workers. No formal educational qualifications are required but employers may give preference to candidates with some GCSEs at grade E or above.

☞ Three-year sandwich course for the BTEC National Diploma in Forestry. Four GCSEs at grades A, B or C are required including English, mathematics and at least a

single award science or a BTEC First Diploma in Land
Based Industries (Forestry). Applicants must be at least 18
and have a minimum of one year's practical experience
before going to college. The BTEC National Diploma can
be followed by the Higher National Diploma course.
Applicants can also enter the HND course with four
GCSEs including English, mathematics and at least single
award science and one A-level in an appropriate subject.
☛ Degree course in forestry. A good base of GCSEs at
grades A, B or C is required for specialisation in science
subjects at A-level. See Higher Education on page 132.
✍ **Further information** Forestry Commission,
Personnel Branch, 231 Corstorphine Road, Edinburgh
EH12 7AT (about careers)
📖 **Reading** *Careers in Forestry* published by and
available free from the Commission
Also see the addresses and publications listed under
Farming
☛ School careers library classification WAF

Fuel Technology
see **Engineering – Energy Engineering**

Funeral Work and Work in Cemeteries and Graveyards

Funeral directors make funeral arrangements, embalmers
prepare bodies for burial or cremation. Cemetery and
graveyard workers administer cremations and burials and
the upkeep of the premises and grounds.
☛ Part-time study for the Diploma in Funeral Directing.
Twelve months' practical experience is needed before
being able to sit the examinations. Part-time study for the
examinations of the National Examinations Board of
Embalmers or the Institute of Burial and Cremation
Administration. For all these examinations GCSEs at
grades A, B or C in English and mathematics exempt

candidates from the preliminary examination.

✍ **Further information** National Association of Funeral Directors, 618 Warwick Road, Solihull, West Midlands B91 1AA

British Institute of Embalmers, Anubis House, 21c Station Road, Knowle, Solihull, West Midlands B93 0HL

Institute of Burial and Cremation Administration, The Gatehouse, Kew Meadow Path, Richmond, Surrey TW9 4EN

National Examinations Board of Embalmers, Huxley House, William Street, Redditch, Worcestershire B97 4AJ

☞ School careers library classification IP

Furniture Design
see **Art and Design**

Gardening
see **Horticulture**

Gas Engineering
see **Engineering**

General Practitioner
see **Medicine and Surgery**

Geology

Geologists study the formation and structure of the materials that make up the earth. This is a small profession and some geologists do pure research – research with no end in view except for increasing man's knowledge of the world. Others work, often abroad, for oil and mining companies that are looking to new sources of minerals while others work as engineering geologists with civil engineering firms.

☞ Three-year degree course in geology. A good base of GCSEs at grades A, B or C for specialisation in science A-levels is required. Three A-levels chosen from geology, physics, chemistry, biological subjects, geography and mathematical subjects are recommended for sixth-form study. Subjects not held at A-level should generally be held at GCSE except for geology which is never formally required for entry to a geology degree course.

✍ **Further information** British Geological Survey, Keyworth, Nottingham NG12 5GG

Institution of Geologists, Geological Society Apartments, Burlington House, Piccadilly, London W1V 9HG

▥ **Reading** *Careers in the Geological Sciences* published by and available free from the British Geological Survey

Geology the Science: Geology the Profession published by and available free from both the Institution and the British Geological Survey

Geological and Environmental Sciences Degree Course Guide published for CRAC by Hobsons Publishing PLC, price £5.95

☛ School careers library classification QOL

Graphic Design
see **Art and Design**

Graphic Reproduction
see **Printing – Printing Crafts**

Hairdressing

Hairdressers cut, shampoo, set, colour and perm hair. Sometimes this career is combined with beauty therapy.

☛ Two-year full-time course at colleges of further education, leading to National Vocational Qualification (NVQ) Level 2. There are no formal entry requirements but many colleges give preference to candidates with some GCSEs at grade E or above preferably in English, mathematics and science.

☛ Two-year day-release course at colleges of further education while working in a hairdresser's salon as an apprentice. Many students enter hairdressing through Youth Training (YT). Entry requirements as above.

✍ **Further information** The Guild of Hairdressers, 24 Woodbridge Road, Guildford, Surrey GU1 1DY (please enclose a stamped addressed envelope)
Hairdressing Training Board, 3 Chequer Road, Doncaster, Yorkshire DN1 2AA

📖 **Reading** *Working In* Series: *Hairdressing and Beauty* published by and available from the Careers and Occupational Information Centre, price £2.35

☛ School careers library classification IL

Health Services Management

Health services managers are non-medical staff who run hospitals, primary care and community health services.

☛ Day-release, evening or correspondence course, supported by activities arranged by regional education committees, for the examinations of the Institute of Health Services Management. Candidates must be working in health service units. Three GCSEs at grades A, B or C and two A-levels are required including English and mathematics or another 'quantitative' science subject. The following subjects are not acceptable: drama, music, photography and textiles.

☛ Various training schemes run by regional health authorities for candidates with relevant qualifications, for example, BTEC National Certificates and Diplomas in Public Administration, accountancy qualifications, etc.

☛ A degree in any subject followed by study programmes leading to the examinations of the Institute of Health Services Management. See Higher Education on page 132.

✍ **Further information** Institute of Health Services Management, 75 Portland Place, London W1N 4AN

☞ School careers library classification CAL

Health Visiting

Health visitors are nurses who work in the community to prevent disease. Their work is with people in all age groups but they concentrate particularly on young children and the old. They visit all mothers with children under five and advise on feeding and other aspects of care. They do not nurse the sick.

☞ One-year full-time course leading to the Health Visitor's Certificate for registered general nurses. Five GCSEs at grades A, B or C or an education entrance test is required. Some training schools may demand specific GCSE subjects and/or A-levels.

☞ Three- or four-year full-time degree course in nursing. A good base of GCSEs at grades A, B or C and at least two A-levels are required. Some universities and colleges specify science A-levels; colleges which do not require science A-levels will require double award science at GCSE. Some degree courses include options leading to the health visitor registration award. If there are no such options the degree course should be followed by a postgraduate course.

✍ **Further information** English National Board for Nursing, Midwifery and Health Visiting, Careers Service, PO Box 356, Sheffield s8 osj

▥ **Reading** *Nursing in the Community (HSC5)* published by the Department of Health and available free from Health Service Careers, PO Box 204, London se5 7es

☞ School careers library classification JAD

Home Economics

The home economist is a professional adviser on food, nutrition, textiles, clothing, home management and design, household services and research related to the home and the community.

☛ Two-year full-time course for the City and Guilds Certificate in Home Economics for Family and Community Care – 794. The course is designed for those who wish to choose employment in which home economics skills are relevant to working with people: with children, the elderly and the mentally and physically disabled. There are no specific educational requirements but for entry the colleges may give preference to candidates with some GCSEs at grade E or above. Certificate holders can become affiliates of the Institute of Home Economics.

☛ Full-time and part-time courses for the BTEC National Diploma/Certificate in Home Economics. Four GCSEs at grades A, B or C or a BTEC First Certificate/Diploma or the City and Guilds Certificate in Home Economics are required for entry.

☛ Two-year full-time course for the BTEC Higher National Diploma in Home Economics. Four GCSEs at grades A, B or C including English and a science and one A-level, another subject having been studied to A-level, are required.

☛ Degree in home economics, food science or nutrition at a university or college of higher education. A good base of GCSEs at grades A, B or C and two A-levels are required. Science subjects and home economics subjects are sometimes required at A-level or at GCSE. If you are intending to become a professional home economist after taking the degree course, you should check with the Institute that the course has the required content of home economics. See Higher Education on page 132.

✍ **Further information** Institute of Home Economics, Aldwych House, 71–91 Aldwych, London WC2B 4HN

▥ **Reading** *Careers in Home Economics* published by and available free from the Institute

Working In Series: *Home Economics* published by and available from the Careers and Occupational Information Centre, price £2.35

☛ School careers library classification ID

Horses, Work With

Grooms work in stables caring for the horses; riding instructors teach children and adults to ride, many people do both.

☛ 18–24 month part-time or full-time course leading to the examinations Horse Knowledge and Riding Stage III and Preliminary Teaching Test of the British Horse Society. Four GCSEs at grades A, B or C including English are required in order to take the test under the age of 17. All GCSE subjects are acceptable. No GCSEs are required if the test is taken over the age of 18.

☛ Full-time college courses for the BTEC National Diploma in Horse Management and similar awards. Four GCSEs at grades A, B or C are required for entry.

Some 16 and 17 year-old leavers enter training through Youth Training (YT). There are no formal entry requirements.

✍ **Further information** British Horse Society, British Equestrian Centre, Stoneleigh, Kenilworth, Warwickshire CV8 2LR

▥ **Reading** *Working with Horses* published by and available from the British Horse Society

Working In Series: *Animals – Work With* published by and available from the Careers and Occupational Information Centre, price £2.65

☛ School careers library classification WAM

Horticulture

There are two main types of horticulture: commercial horticulture, which is growing fruit, vegetables, cut flowers and plants for sale; and amenity horticulture which is work in parks and gardens and the maintenance of sports grounds and golf courses.

☛ Most 16 and 17 year-old school-leavers enter the industry through Youth Training (YT) schemes which are managed either by local agricultural and horticultural colleges or by other approved training organisations. The one- and two-year schemes offer planned work experience on horticultural holdings and vocational education and training through day and block release courses which generally lead to National Vocational Qualifications at Levels 1 and 2 in either Commercial or Amenity Horticulture. There are no specific entry requirements but preference may be given to candidates who have some GCSEs at grades E or above.

☛ One-year full-time course for the National Certificate in Horticulture (Amenity or Commercial). No formal entry qualifications are necessary but GCSEs at grade E or above in English, mathematics and science are desirable. The minimum age is 17 and one year's practical experience is required; this may be a full-time introductory course in horticulture or a YT programme which includes eight months' practical experience. This National Certificate course can be followed by a supplementary one-year full-time course for the Advanced National Certificate in Horticulture or a BTEC National Diploma.

☛ Three-year sandwich course for the BTEC National Diploma in Commercial or Amenity Horticulture or in specialised sections of these subjects. Four GCSEs at grades A, B or C including a subject testing command of English and either mathematics and single award science or double award science are required. Minimum age 17 (some colleges may require 18 minimum) and at least one year's practical experience is also required.

☛ Part-time study to help those employed in full-time practical horticulture who are taking the 'Master of Horticulture' examinations administered by the Royal Horticultural Society. Applicants are expected to have two A-levels including one science subject or their equivalent as the examinations are at a level equivalent to a university degree. At least three years' practical experience is required.

☛ Three-year sandwich course for the BTEC Higher National Diploma in Horticulture. Four GCSEs at grades A, B or C including a subject testing command of English and two distinct mathematics/science subjects, one A-level and another subject studied at A-level are required. The A-level pass must be one of the following: biology, botany, chemistry, computer studies, economics, engineering science, environmental studies, geography, geology, human biology, mathematics (any), physical science, physics, physics-with-chemistry, zoology. Candidates may also enter with BTEC National Diplomas in science, agriculture or horticulture.

☛ Three- or four-year degree course in horticulture. A good base of GCSEs at grades A, B or C with future specialisation in A-level science subjects is required. Chemistry and a biological subject are the preferred A-level subjects. See Higher Education on page 132.

✍ **Further information** The Senior Scientist, Royal Horticultural Society, RHS Garden, Wisley, Woking, Surrey GU23 6QB

Institute of Horticulture, PO Box 313, 80 Vincent Square, London SW1P 2PE

The Local Government Management Board, Arndale House, Arndale Centre, Luton, Bedfordshire LU1 2TS (Training Scheme)

▥ **Reading** *Come into Horticulture* and an information sheet on courses published by and available free from the Institute of Horticulture, please enclose a stamped addressed envelope

Please see the addresses and publications listed under 'Farming'

☛ School careers library classification WAD

Hotels
see **Catering**

Housing Management

Housing managers work for housing organisations including local authorities, housing associations, housing charities and trusts. They are involved in allocation, maintaining and planning rented accommodation. They must know about the structure of buildings, landlord and tenant law, and planning.

☛ Three-year part-time programme for the BTEC National Certificate in Housing Studies for which four GCSEs at grades A, B or C are required. This can be followed by the Higher National Certificate in Housing Studies which can also be entered with candidates holding one A-level. There are distance learning versions of the BTEC National and Higher National Certificate from the NALGO Correspondence Institute. Students can then take the Professional Diploma in Housing. This route takes about six years to become professionally qualified.

☛ Four-year sandwich or three-year full-time degree course in housing which is recognised by the Institute. A good base of GCSEs and at least two A-levels are required for entry. It is also possible to take these degree courses part-time.

☛ Degree in any subject followed by a one-year postgraduate course or three-year day-release courses for the Graduate Foundation Course and the Professional Diploma in Housing. See Higher Education on page 132.

✍ **Further information** Institute of Housing, Octavia House, Westwood Business Park, Westwood Way, Coventry, West Midlands CV4 8JP

▥ **Reading** *A Career in Housing* and a *Guide to Professional Qualification* published by and available free from the Institute

☛ School careers library classification UM

Industrial Design
see **Art and Design**

Information Science

Information scientists (also called information officers) collect and organise information about their organisation's work. They are involved in the whole process of information handling including abstracting, report writing, literature searches and information retrieval. The use of computers is an integral part of modern practice. There can be considerable overlap between the work done by information scientists and librarians, see page 249.

☞ A degree course in information science (very few available). A good base of GCSEs at grades A, B or C including mathematics, science and a foreign language and two A-levels are required.

☞ A degree in any subject, but preference is often given to candidates with degrees in scientific or technological subjects, followed by a postgraduate course in information science or an allied subject. See Higher Education on page 132.

☞ Both the Institute of Information Scientists and the Library Association accredit several degree and postgraduate courses in common for entry to professional membership. Employers will accept graduates from these courses for appointment to professional posts across the spectrum of library and information science.

✍ **Further information** Institute of Information Scientists, 44 Museum Street, London WC1A 1LY
The Education Department, The Library Association, 7 Ridgmount Street, London WC1E 7AE

📖 **Reading** *A Career in Information Science* published by and available free from the Institute

Various careers leaflets published by and available from
the Library Association
☛ School careers library classification FAF

Institutional Management
see **Catering**

Insurance

Insurance is a means by which many people pay small
sums into a common fund, and then if some misfortune
occurs such as an accident they can be compensated for
their loss. Brokers act as intermediaries between the
insurance companies and people wanting insurance. Most
insurance companies have separate departments covering
marine, aviation, motor, life, property and accident.

☛ Three- or four-year part-time courses for the
Institute's Associateship examination followed by about
two years' part-time study for the Institute's Fellowship
Examination. Three A-levels are required or two A-levels
and two GCSEs at grades A, B or C provided that one
subject is English and that one of the A-levels is from the
following list: English, natural sciences, economics, public
and economic affairs, British Constitution, surveying,
accounting (or principles of accounts), sociology, general
principles of English law, business studies, general studies,
religious knowledge. There is a special scheme for
entrants over 20: details from the Institute.

☛ Full-time or part-time college courses for the BTEC
National Certificate/Diploma in Business and Finance for
which four GCSEs at grades A, B or C including English
and preferably mathematics or a BTEC First Certificate
are required for entry. This should be followed by study
for the Institute's Associateship and Fellowship
examinations.

☛ A degree or BTEC Higher National Diploma in any
subject followed by study for the Institute's examinations.

Candidates with certain degrees, for example business studies, may gain subject-for-subject exemptions.

✍ **Further information** Chartered Insurance Institute, Careers Department, 31 Hillcrest Road, South Woodford, London E18 2JP

The British Insurance and Investment Brokers' Association, BIIBA House, 14 Bevis Marks, London EC3A 7NT

📖 **Reading** Booklets published by and available free from the Chartered Insurance Institute

☛ School careers library classification NAG

Interior Decoration and Design
see **Art and Design**

Interpreting
see **Language Work**

Jewellery
see **Retail Distribution** *and* **Art and Design**

Journalism

Journalists work on provincial and national newspapers and on magazines. They work as reporters, as feature writers producing articles on special topics and as specialists in areas such as sport or finance. Competition is extremely keen and successful entrants not only have the necessary academic qualifications but often show an interest in journalism by having written articles for school or college magazines and newspapers.

☛ A period of probation is usually followed by a training contract on a regional or local newspaper. The qualification period for taking the test is two years. During the qualification period trainees attend college and are expected to pass examinations in law, public administration and shorthand. Minimum entry requirements are normally five GCSEs at grades A, B or C including English but A-levels are usually required. All GCSE and A-level subjects are acceptable.

☛ Full-time one-year course followed by probation and a training contract on a regional or local newspaper. The qualifying period for entry for the National Certificate is 18 months. Two A-levels are required for entry to the one-year course.

☛ Degree in any subject. Graduates serve a period of probation and have a training contract. The qualifying period for entry for the National Certificate is 18 months. There are some one-year postgraduate courses in journalism. See Higher Education on page 132.

✍ **Further information** Training Department, Newspaper Society, Bloomsbury House, Bloomsbury Square, 74–77 Great Russell Street, London WC1B 3DA (please send an A4 stamped addressed envelope)

▥ **Reading** *Working In* Series: *Journalism* published by and available from the Careers and Occupational Information Centre, price £2.65

☛ School careers library classification FAC

Laboratory Technician Work

Laboratory technicians and assistants maintain the equipment in a scientific laboratory and set up experiments. They may take readings, mix chemical solutions, prepare slides and trouble shoot experiments before they are used by classes in educational institutions. A technician may be an integral part of a research team carrying out skilled techniques within criteria laid down by professional scientists. See also Medical laboratory science work.

☞ Full-time or part-time college courses for a BTEC National Certificate/Diploma in Science. Four GCSEs at grades A, B or C including mathematics and preferably double award science or a BTEC First Certificate/Diploma in Science is required.

✍ **Further information** Institute of Science Technology, Mansell House, 22 Bore Street, Lichfield, Staffordshire ws13 6lp

📖 **Reading** Factsheets on courses in science published by and available free from the Business and Technology Education Council, Central House, Upper Woburn Place, London wc1h 0hh

☞ School careers library classification Q

Land Management
see **Estate Agency** *and* **Surveying**

Landscape Architecture

Landscape architects design the layout of open spaces – these might be parks and playgrounds or the land surrounding public buildings, power stations or factories. They advise on the planting of trees and shrubs in such developments.

☞ Four-year full-time or five-year sandwich course leading to a degree in landscape architecture. Candidates require three GCSEs at grades A, B or C and two A-levels, most colleges require English, mathematics or science; other useful subjects would be art, history, biology/botany, geography/geology and a language other than English.

☞ A good base of GCSEs and at least two A-levels are required for a degree in architecture, planning or a related discipline followed by a postgraduate course. See Higher Education on page 132.

✍ **Further information** The Landscape Institute, 6/7 Barnard Mews, London sw11 1qu

📖 **Reading** *Professional Careers in Landscape Architecture, Landscape Sciences and Landscape Management* published by the Landscape Institute. Single copies available free
Architecture, Landscape Architecture and Planning Degree Course Guide published by Hobsons Publishing PLC, price £5.95
☛ School careers library classification UL

Land Surveying
see **Surveying**

Language Work

Translators translate written material generally into their own language. Knowledge of another language by itself is not sufficient; they must in addition have some specialised knowledge – of business, science, building, engineering or law.

Simultaneous interpreters translate while a person is speaking, usually translating into their own language. Liaison interpreters translate into and out of two or three languages being used in a discussion. Interpretation is a very small field.

Bilingual secretaries work in many commercial firms translating letters and orders and writing letters in foreign languages. In firms that do not employ translators they may do some translation.

Other careers where languages are useful or essential: exporting, air cabin crew, marketing, hotel and catering (see Catering), tourism (see Travel), Civil Service (Diplomatic Service, Home Office), Armed Forces, teaching foreign languages and international telephone operation (GCSE French required).

☛ Full-time secretarial linguist course; qualifications to enter these courses range from three GCSEs at grades A, B or C to three A-levels including two A-level languages.

☛ Full-time or part-time college courses for a BTEC National Certificate/Diploma in Business and Finance. Four GCSEs at grades A, B or C or a BTEC First Certificate/Diploma is required for entry. The National awards can be followed by a BTEC Higher National Diploma or college diploma course in business studies with language options, languages for business or similar courses. These courses can also be entered with three GCSEs at grades A, B or C and one A-level.

☛ A good base of GCSEs at grades A, B or C including English leading to A-levels which include at least one in a foreign language. A few universities prefer one of the GCSEs to be Latin. Although it is possible to enter a degree course in foreign languages without A-level or AS-levels in languages this is rare. Some degree courses in modern languages concentrate on literature while others deal with the social and economic life of the country. See Higher Education on page 132.

✍ **Further information** Institute of Linguists, 24a Highbury Grove, London N5 2EA

⌁ **Reading** *Working In* Series: *Languages* published by and available from the Careers and Occupational Information Centre, price £2.35

CRAC Degree Course Guides: *French; Italian and Hispanic Studies; Russian and Oriental Studies (including African Studies); German (including Dutch and Scandinavian Studies)* published by Hobsons Publishing PLC, price £5.95 each

☛ School careers library classification FAL

Law
see **Legal Work**

Leather Technology

Leather technologists apply their scientific knowledge of chemistry, physics and biology to the processes of converting hides and skins into finished leathers. These leathers are then used in other industries to produce shoes, clothes, gloves, leather goods, safety products, sports equipment and industrial leathers.

☞ Open learning courses leading to the City and Guilds Operatives' Certificate in leather manufacture and the City and Guilds Craft Certificate in leather manufacture. There are no formal entry qualifications required.

☞ Two-year block-release course for the BTEC National Certificate in leather technology. Four GCSEs at grades A, B or C including chemistry, physics, mathematics and English or a BTEC First Certificate/Diploma is required for entry.

☞ Three-year full-time course for a degree in leather technology at the British School of Leather Technology, Nene College, Northampton. Four GCSEs including mathematics and biology and A-level chemistry or the BTEC National Certificate are required for entry.

☞ Entry after a degree in chemistry or a suitable postgraduate course. Graduates in chemistry, chemical engineering or biochemistry may study for a degree in leather technology in one or two years or for the Associateship of the Leathersellers' Centre by research. For a degree in chemistry a good base of GCSEs at grades A, B or C and normally A-levels in mathematics, physics and chemistry are required. See Higher Education on page 132.

✍ **Further information** The British School of Leather Technology, Nene College, Moulton Park, Northampton NN2 7AL

☞ School careers library classification SAF

Legal Work

Barristers represent their clients in court. As well as advocacy they do paper work – giving their opinion on legal matters. Clients cannot approach a barrister direct; they must do so through a solicitor.

☛ A good base of GCSEs at grades A, B or C and two or more A-levels are required for entry to a degree course (not necessarily in law). It is essential to have a first or second class honours degree in any subject. Graduates with non-law degrees must first take the one-year course for the Common Professional Examination. Everyone intending to practise at the Bar of England and Wales must then attend the one-year vocational course at the Inns of Court School of Law. Students reading for the Bar must join one of the four Inns of Court before starting the vocational stage of training and keep the required number of dining terms in their Inn of Court (ie eating a certain number of dinners at the Inn of Court they have joined). A newly qualified barrister must then spend a year as a pupil in the chambers of a practising barrister and may not do any professional work until the second six months. See Higher Education on page 132.

✍ **Further information** The Council of Legal Education, Inns of Court School of Law, 39 Eagle Street, London WC1R 4AJ

▥ **Reading** *The Bar into the '90s* published by and available free from the General Council of the Bar, 3 Bedford Row, London WC1R 4AJ

☛ School careers library classification LAB

Legal executives work in solicitors' offices and legal departments and usually specialise in a particular area of work – divorce, litigation (taking cases to court), conveyancing (buying and selling houses), or wills and probate (dealing with matters when someone dies). They interview clients and submit papers to court. They do not represent clients in court.

☛ Part-time, day-release or evening classes at a college of further education for the Institute's examinations. Four academic GCSEs at grades A, B or C including English are required. Practical subjects such as art, drama, food and nutrition, technology, textiles and woodwork may not be acceptable as it depends on the syllabus covered; further details from the Institute. For students without four GCSEs there are one-year part-time courses for the Preliminary Certificate in Legal Studies. To qualify as a legal executive applicants must be working in a legal department or a solicitor's office.

✍ **Further information** Institute of Legal Executives, Kempston Manor, Kempston, Bedford MK42 7AB

📖 **Reading** *Opening the Way to a Career in Law* and *From School to a Career in Law* published by and available free from the Institute

☛ School careers library classification LAD

Solicitors carry out a wide range of legal work, and normally act on the instructions of clients. Clients can ask for any legal service, from buying a home to selling a company. A solicitor's role is to give legal advice and representation, and matters can vary from crime to conveyancing, from making a will to carrying out a multi-million pound deal. At present solicitors represent their clients in the lower courts, hiring a barrister for representation in the higher courts, but in due course solicitors will have the right of representation in the higher courts.

☛ A good base of GCSEs at grades A, B or C and at least two A-levels are required for a degree in any subject. This should be followed by a one-year course for the Common Professional Examination (or equivalent), a further year for the new Legal Practice Course and then two years in a Training Contract with a firm of solicitors or other approved organisation. See Higher Education on page 132.

☛ A good base of GCSEs at grades A, B or C and normally three A-levels at high grades (subjects rarely specified) for a law degree. The degree should be followed by the new one-year Legal Practice Course and then two years in a Training Contract with a firm of solicitors or other approved organisation. See Higher Education on page 132.

☛ It is possible to qualify as a solicitor after working as a fully qualified legal executive. Candidates who are over 25 and have worked for five years in a solicitor's office and have Fellowship status of the Institute of Legal Executives can either take the Legal Practice course or can enter two-year training and take the Legal Practice course externally.

✍ **Further information** The Law Society, 113 Chancery Lane, London WC2A 1PL

The Law Society's Careers and Recruitment Service, 227/228 Strand, London WC2R 1BA

▥ **Reading** Solicitors – *A Career for Tomorrow* published by and available free from the Law Society's Careers and Recruitment Service

☛ School careers library classification LAC

Library and Information Management

Professional entry

Librarians and information professionals are responsible for selecting, buying, organising and using all kinds of materials and media which record information. They work in public libraries, schools, universities, colleges, industry and commerce, the media, national libraries and museums – in fact for any organisation that has information needs. The use of computers is integral to modern practice. See also Information Science.

☛ Three- or four-year Library Association accredited university or college of higher education degree course in information studies. A good base of GCSEs at grades A, B or C and at least two A-levels or a BTEC National award are normally required for entry.

☛ A degree in any subject followed by a one-year Library Association accredited postgraduate course in information studies. See Higher Education on page 132. Graduates may then work towards gaining the professional qualifications offered by the Library

Association through the award of Chartered Membership and entry to its Professional Register.

Para–professional entry
Library and information assistants support library and information managers by carrying out the more routine work. Many assistants are not qualified but can study for vocational qualifications whilst in post.

☛ Full-time or part-time college courses for a BTEC National Certificate/Diploma in Business and Finance with options in library and information work. Four GCSEs at grades A, B or C including English and mathematics are required for entry. Alternatively the City and Guilds Library Assistants' Certificate or a BTEC First Certificate/Diploma will be accepted for entry. With a BTEC National Award with appropriate options it will be possible to be considered for degree courses in librarianship on a par with A-level holders.

✍ **Further information** The Library Association, 7 Ridgmount Street, London WC1E 7AE

▥ **Reading** Various career leaflets published by and available from the Library Association

☛ School careers library classification FAF

Local Government Administration

People working in local government administration are employed by local authorities who run a wide range of public services including museums, libraries, education, refuse collection and street cleaning, parks, social services, swimming pools and sports centres. Increasingly local authority services are being put out to tender so that private firms can compete for the work. Many professional posts in local authorities are dealt with under the appropriate career: these include accountancy, social work, planning, housing management and environmental health.

Administrative Grade

☛ Full-time or part-time college courses for a BTEC National Certificate/Diploma in Public Administration or Business and Finance. Four GCSEs at grades A, B or C including English and mathematics or a BTEC First Certificate/Diploma is required for entry. This can be followed by a part-time course for the BTEC Higher National Certificate in public administration options. These courses can also be entered with three GCSEs at grades A, B or C and one A-level.

☛ Two-year full-time or three-year sandwich course for the BTEC Higher National Diploma in Public Administration. Three GCSEs at grades A, B or C and one A-level or a BTEC National Award are required for entry.

☛ Degree in any subject for entry to administrative trainee schemes run by local authorities. Some authorities may prefer trainees who have taken degrees such as public administration. See Higher Education on page 132.

Clerical Grade

☛ One-year part-time course for the BTEC First Certificate or one-year full-time or two-year part-time course for the BTEC First Diploma in Business and Finance. There are no formal entry requirements but many colleges require two or three GCSEs at grade E or above including English. Many local authorities lay down entry requirements of GCSEs at grades A, B or C for the clerical grade.

✍ **Further information** The Local Government Management Board, Arndale House, Arndale Centre, Luton, Bedfordshire LU1 2TS

▥ **Reading** Leaflets published by and available free from the Local Government Management Board

☛ School careers library classification CAG

Marine Engineering
see **Engineering**

Marines
see **Royal Navy and Royal Marines**

Marketing

Marketing managers find out what potential customers wish to buy, develop products or services to cater for this and plan and co-ordinate the work of the various departments of a company to make the product or service available at the right price.

☛ Two-year part-time course for the Qualifying Certificate of the Institute of Marketing. Students must be at least 18 and have one A-level and four GCSEs at grades A, B or C including English and a numeracy subject; other suitable subjects would be single or double award science, history, geography, economics, business studies and foreign languages. All subjects are acceptable. This can be followed by a further year's study for entry to the Diploma of the Institute. Alternative qualifications for entry to the Diploma course include BTEC Higher awards in Business and Finance with a marketing orientation or a degree.

☛ Part-time or full-time college courses for the BTEC National Certificate/Diploma in Business and Finance. Four GCSEs at grades A, B or C preferably including English and mathematics or a BTEC First Certificate/Diploma is required for entry. This can be followed by BTEC Higher awards with marketing options and/or professional qualifications.

☛ A degree in any subject followed by a graduate traineeship or a degree in business studies with marketing options followed by a traineeship. Marketing degrees are now being offered by some higher education institutions. A good base of GCSEs at grades A, B or C and at least two A-levels are required to enter a degree course. See Higher Education on page 132.

✍ **Further information** The Chartered Institute of Marketing, Moor Hall, Cookham, Berkshire SL6 9QH

▥ **Reading** *Working In* Series: *Marketing* published by and available from the Careers and Occupational Information Centre, price £2.35

☛ School careers library classification OB

Market Research

Market researchers find out what consumers want and why. They want to know the demand that exists for their products and services; how their products compare with competitors'; how different types of advertising and packaging affect sales. There are many ways of collecting this information: the best known is by interviewing the public. Trained interviewers are employed on a part-time basis. Research executives guide the project through its various stages, designing the questionnaire and analysing and reporting the findings.

☛ A good base of GCSEs at grades A, B or C including mathematics and two or more A-levels are required. Most executive-level posts require a degree in any subject. There are openings for market research assistants with GCSEs and A-levels. See Higher Education on page 132.

✍ **Further information** Market Research Society, 15 Northburgh Street, London EC1V 0AH

▥ **Reading** *A Career in Market Research* and *What is Market Research?* published by and available free from the Society

☛ School careers library classification OB

Materials Science and Metallurgy

Materials scientists apply the science of physics and chemistry to all materials – metal and non-metals. They work both in the production of the material and its processing into finished products. Metallurgists are concerned with the extraction of metals from their ores, and the composition and uses of metals and alloys. Other materials scientists apply similar principles to other materials particularly polymers, ceramics and glass.

In 1992 the Plastics and Rubber Institute and the Ceramics Institute merged with the Institute of Metals to form the Institute of Materials.

Materials Science Technician

☞ Full-time or part-time college course for a BTEC National Certificate/Diploma in Metals Technology or Materials Technology. Four GCSEs at grades A, B or C including mathematics and at least single award science or a BTEC First Certificate/Diploma are required for entry. The BTEC National Certificate can be followed by a two-year part-time course for the Higher National Certificate or a four-year part-time or three-year sandwich course for the Higher National Diploma.

Materials Technologist/Metallurgist

☞ Two-year full-time, three-year sandwich course or four-year part-time course for the BTEC Higher National Diploma in Metals Technology or Materials Technology. Candidates require either a BTEC National Certificate/Diploma with appropriate units or A-level study of chemistry and physics with a pass in one of these subjects and a GCSE at grade A, B or C in mathematics. Holders of the BTEC Higher National Diploma qualify for the Associateship of the Institute.

☞ Degree in metallurgy or materials science. A good base of GCSEs at grades A, B or C is required. A-levels in physics, chemistry and mathematics are generally required. See Higher Education on page 132 about entry to higher education. With an accredited classified honours degree in metallurgy or materials science the holder can become a Corporate Member of the Institute.

✍ **Further information** The Institute of Materials, PO Box 471, 1 Carlton House Terrace, London SW1Y 5DB
☛ School careers library classification QOS

Mathematics

Mathematicians are employed to solve problems in engineering, computing, medicine, economics, marketing, physics and statistics and to analyse mathematical data. Most routine work is done by computers.

☛ Two-year full-time or three-year sandwich course for the BTEC Higher National Diploma in mathematics, statistics and computing. An A-level pass in mathematics with at least 50% pure mathematics content and an adequate command of English are required or a BTEC National Certificate/Diploma with appropriate modules.

☛ A good base of GCSEs at grades A, B or C and at least two A-levels preferably including more than one mathematics A-level are required for a degree in mathematics. See Higher Education on page 132.

✍ **Further information** Institute of Mathematics and its Applications, 16 Nelson Street, Southend-on-Sea, Essex SS1 1EF

Mathematical Association, 259 London Road, Leicester LE2 3BE

▥ **Reading** *Qualifications and Careers in Mathematics* published by and available from the Institute of Mathematics and its Applications, price £8.00
Careers for the Mathematically Qualified published by and available free from the Mathematical Association

Working In Series: *Mathematics* published by and available from the Careers and Occupational Information Centre, price £2.50

☛ School careers library classification QOG

Mechanical Engineering
see **Engineering**

Medical Laboratory Science Work

Medical laboratory scientific officers work in hospital pathology and other medical laboratories. They analyse blood, study tissues removed in operations, study bacteria and viruses and undertake chemical analysis of urine and body fluids.

It is likely that in the next few years the medical laboratory science work will become a graduate-only profession. This will make the HNC/HND courses no longer relevant for the profession.

☛ Three-year sandwich course for the BTEC Higher National Diploma in medical laboratory sciences. Three GCSEs at grades A, B or C and one A-level and another subject having been studied to A-level are required. One of the A-level subjects must be chemistry. A BTEC National Certificate or Diploma in Science with appropriate units is an alternative entry qualification. The BTEC Higher National Certificate is a two-year part-time course and has similar entry qualifications to the BTEC Higher National Diploma. See note about graduate entry above.

☛ A good base of GCSEs at grades A, B or C leading to specialisation in A-level science subjects is required to enter an accredited degree course in biomedical sciences. These courses provide exemption from the first year of the three-year Fellowship programme of the Institute. A list of these courses is available from the Institute. Degree courses where the principal subject is animal physiology, biochemistry, biology, chemistry, microbiology, physics or zoology can be followed by study for the Fellowship of the Institute. All the degree courses must be approved by the Medical Laboratory Scientific Officers Board at the Council for Professions Supplementary to Medicine. See Higher Education on page 132.

✍ **Further information** Institute of Medical Laboratory Sciences, 12 Queen Anne Street, London W1M 0AU

▥ **Reading** Leaflets published by and available free from the Institute

☛ School careers library classification JAX

Medical Records Work

Medical records officers compile and maintain medical records in hospitals and health centres.

☛ Part-time, day-release or correspondence course for the Diploma examinations of the Association. To take the Diploma five GCSEs at grades A, B or C are required including English and mathematics. The following subjects are not acceptable: child development, drama, electronics, engineering, music, and photography.

✍ **Further information** Association of Health Care Information and Medical Records Officers, Pear Tree Cottage, Mill Lane, Horsemans Green, Whitchurch, Shropshire SY13 3EA

▥ **Reading** *A Worthwhile Career in Health Care Information and Medical Records* published by and available free from the Association; a stamped addressed envelope is required if requesting information

☛ School careers library classification CAV

Medicine and Surgery

Doctors diagnose and treat physical and mental disorders. They can work as general practitioners (GPs) running surgeries and visiting patients in their own homes or can work in hospitals where they specialise in a medical field such as paediatrics (child health), geriatrics (medical care of old people), psychiatry (mental health) or surgery (operations). A few doctors work in community health where the emphasis is on preventing disease.

☛ A good base of GCSEs at grades A, B or C including English, mathematics and double award science followed by A-levels which should include chemistry. Fewer than half the medical schools now insist on three A-level science subjects including chemistry. It would be wise to plan to study physics and biology beyond the level of double award science – by taking these subjects at A/S level, for example. A five-year degree course is essential to qualify as a doctor; practical hospital experience is also required. See Higher Education on page 132.

✍ **Further information** British Medical Association, Tavistock Square, London WC1H 9JP
Information sheets available on request from the British Medical Association (please send a large stamped addressed envelope)

▥ **Reading** *Learning Medicine* published by and available from the British Medical Association, price £4.95
Medicine Degree Course Guide published by Hobsons Publishing PLC, price £5.95

☛ School careers library classification JAB

Merchant Navy

Deck Officers navigate the ship and are responsible for loading and unloading the cargo.
Engineer Officers operate and maintain the ship's engines.
Electro-Technical/Radio Officers operate and maintain the ship's radio and radar; vacancies are limited.
Ratings are able seamen who work under the direction of the officers. Shipping companies while recruiting British officers often recruit ratings from overseas.

Catering ratings prepare food for members of the crew.

In 1988 a new scheme of assistance for training was introduced by the Department of Transport to increase the number of officers being trained for service in the Merchant Navy.

Deck Officers

All deck officer cadets must be in good health and have good eyesight.

☛ Three-and-a-half-year sandwich course with periods of on-the-job training on board ship and periods of study in approved nautical colleges leading to the BTEC National Diploma in Nautical Science together with the Department of Transport Class 4 Certificate of Competency and ultimately a Higher National Diploma. Four GCSEs at grades A, B or C including mathematics, double award science, English or a subject testing command of English are required. Entry is as a deck officer with a shipping company.

☛ A scheme similar to the BTEC Diploma course leads directly to the Department of Transport Class 3 Certificate of Competency. For this, candidates require three GCSEs at grades A, B or C and to have studied two A-levels and obtained a pass in one. One A-level must be mathematics or a physical science.

☛ Three-year full-time to four- to six-year sandwich course leading to a degree in nautical studies. Three GCSEs at grades A, B or C and two A-levels are the minimum requirement. Some colleges require mathematics and physics at A-level. All require some evidence of study of both these subjects beyond GCSE, eg A/S level.

☛ Other schemes exist for which the minimum entry requirement is three GCSEs at grade E or above in mathematics, science and a subject testing command of English.

Engineer Officers

☛ A sandwich course with periods of on-the-job

training on board ship and periods of study in approved colleges and engineering workshops is taken. Successful completion of this course enables students to study for the BTEC Higher National Certificate or Diploma in Marine Engineering. The BTEC awards provide certain exemptions from the Department of Transport Engineers Class 2 Certificate and in certain cases from parts of the Engineers Class 1 Certificate. A minimum of four GCSEs at grades A, B or C including mathematics and science are required for entry to the Higher National Certificate course. For entry to the Higher National Diploma course one A-level in either mathematics or physics is also required, the other A-level subject having been studied to this level but not necessarily passed. Entry is as an engineer officer cadet with a shipping company. The holder of the Department of Transport Engineers Second Class Certificate can register as a Technician Engineer with the Engineering Council, the holder of a First Class Certificate can register as an Incorporated Engineer and the holder of the Extra First Class Certificate can register as a Chartered Engineer. See Engineering.

Dual Certificate Officer (Deck and Engineer)
☛ Four- to five-year sandwich course with periods at sea and periods at nautical college. Four GCSEs at grades A, B or C in mathematics, double award science and a subject testing command of English and mathematics and physics studied to A-level and a pass in one are required.

Electro-Technical Officer/Radio Officer
☛ Three-year full-time course at an approved college. After the second year successful students gain the BTEC National Diploma in Marine Radio and Radar; after the third year the BTEC Higher National Certificate in Marine Radio and Radar. Three GCSEs at grades A, B or C in mathematics, science and English are generally required for entry. Candidates cannot go to sea until they have successfully completed the course.

Junior Deck, Engine Room and Catering Ratings

☛ Shipping company sponsorship is essential before enrolment at the National Sea Training College, Gravesend. This formerly single sex college now has an intake of 10% women and trains future seamen/women and stewards, the latter with progression to ship's cook. There are no academic entry requirements but shipping companies normally expect candidates to have GCSEs at grade D or above in mathematics, science and a subject testing command of English. Applicants must be in good health (and have good eyesight for the deck department). There are no longer any age limits.

✍ **Further information** Individual shipping companies, whose addresses can be obtained from the Annual Directory of Shipowners, Shipbuilders and Marine Engineers (The Blue Book) which should be available in large public libraries. The names and addresses of the companies participating in the training scheme can be obtained from the Co-ordinating Agent, Government Assistance for Training, 30/32 St Mary Axe, London EC3A 8ET

☛ School careers library classification YAL

Metallurgy
see **Materials Science and Metallurgy**

Meteorology

Meteorologists provide weather information and carry out research into the atmosphere. The main employer is the Meteorological Office which is a government department.

☛ For entry as an Assistant Scientific Officer a minimum of four GCSEs at grades A, B or C including English and physics/double award science or mathematics (preferably both) are required. Study concessions leading to higher

qualifications such as the BTEC Higher National
Certificate may be granted to suitable staff.

☛ For entry as a Scientific Officer a degree (BTEC
Higher National Diploma or Certificate may possibly be
acceptable) in mathematics, physics, meteorology,
computer science or electronics is required. In general
these courses require a good base of GCSEs at grades A, B
or C and at least two A-levels in mathematics and physics.
See Higher Education on page 132. For both Assistant
Scientific Officer and Scientific Officer posts most
successful applicants have qualifications above the
minimum.

✍ **Further information** Meteorological Office
Recruitment, London Road, Bracknell, Berkshire RG12 2SZ

☛ School careers library classification QOL

Midwifery

A midwife works with expectant mothers in the ante-
natal clinic that mothers attend before the baby is born.
The midwife delivers the baby – unless there are
complications, when a doctor is called. Generally babies
are delivered in hospital but there are a few home births.
The midwife then looks after the mother and the newly
born baby for not less than 10 days, and sometimes up to
the limit of 28 days.

☛ Three-year full-time course for those without
previous nursing experience. Five GCSEs at grades A, B or
C including English and at least single award science are
required. The demand for places is such that
qualifications above the minimum are often necessary.
Minimum age is 17 1/2.

☛ Eighteen months' full-time course for registered
general nurses (see Nursing). The majority of midwives
qualify in this way.

☛ Four-year degree course combining nursing and
midwifery qualifications. Three GCSEs at grades A, B or

C in English, mathematics and at least single award science and two A-levels are required.

✍ **Further information** English National Board for Nursing, Midwifery and Health Visiting, Careers Advisory Centre, PO Box 356, Sheffield s8 0sj

▥ **Reading** *Registered Midwife (HSC3)* published by the Department of Health and available free from Health Service Careers, PO Box 204, London se5 7es

☛ School careers library classification JAD

Mine Engineering
see **Engineering**

Mine Surveying
see **Surveying**

Museum Work

People working in museums and art galleries organise, acquire, catalogue and display the exhibits. They may put on special exhibitions, run museum clubs for children or liaise with schools. Some curators are allowed time to do their own research work. Conservation officers repair and restore exhibits.

☛ On-the-job training as museum assistant. Recruitment to the large national museums was formerly carried out by the Civil Service and there were standard entry requirements. National museums now recruit their own personnel and there are no nationally laid down requirements. Normally museums would be expecting four GCSEs at grades A, B or C as a minimum; in practice most successful candidates have degrees.

☛ Two-year full-time college course for a BTEC Higher National Diploma in Conservation Studies. A foundation course in art and design, a BTEC National award or exceptionally one A-level is required for entry. Three-year full-time degree course in conservation, candidates straight from school require a minimum of two A-levels and a range of GCSEs at grades A, B, or C. These courses lead to posts as conservation officers in museums for which there are few vacancies.

☛ A degree in any subject (competition for posts is keen and subjects such as history of art, social history, arts administration, archaeology, zoology and geology may be preferred). This can be followed either by a one-year university postgraduate course in museum studies or by direct entry.

☛ The Museums Assocation Diploma is being phased out. The Museum Training Institute has been set up to offer flexible training. Successful completion will lead to to the MTI Certificate of Competence which will be validated by the National Council for Vocational Qualifications.

✍ **Further information** Museums Association, 42 Clerkenwell Close, London EC1R OPA
Museum Training Institute, 55 Well Street, Bradford BD1 5PS

▥ **Reading** *Careers in Museums* published by and available free from the Museums Association or Museum Training Institute (please send a large stamped addressed envelope)

☛ School careers library classification FAG

Music

Professional musicians work as composers, performers – playing instruments, singing and conducting – and teachers. Performers may work in large orchestras or in small groups. This is a highly competitive career.

☛ Two- to four-year full-time course at a music college. Entrance is by competitive audition, although in practice most successful candidates will also have a good base of GCSEs at grades A, B or C and one or more A-levels. If the student wishes to combine musical performance and teaching in a state school, GCSEs at grades A, B or C in English and mathematics are required.

☛ Three-year full-time course for a degree in music, a degree where music is combined with other subjects or a performing arts degree. A good base of GCSEs at grades A, B or C and at least two A-levels are required. A-level music is usually required for a degree in music.

✍ **Further information** Incorporated Society of Musicians (ISM), 10 Stratford Place, London win 9ae (careers only)

📖 **Reading** *Careers with Music* published by and available free from the Incorporated Society of Musicians (ISM)

Working In Series: *Music* published by and available from the Careers and Occupational Information Centre, price £2.65

☛ School careers library classification GAD

Nature Conservation

Assistant Regional Officers in English Nature work to preserve plant and animal life; they survey and assess the priorities in their area, liaise with local planning authorities and give advice to schools. **Wardens** undertake practical conservation work in nature reserves and liaise with neighbouring landowners. These are very popular careers and there is strong competition for the few vacancies. There are also posts, often seasonal, working for nature organisations.

Assistant Regional Officers
☛ A good base of GCSEs at grades A, B or C and A-levels in the biological sciences, environmental science or geography are required for entry to a degree in the biological sciences, horticulture, ecology or

environmental sciences which is essential. See Higher
Education on page 132.

Wardens

☛ On-the-job training. Minimum age 26. Candidates
should be keen naturalists interested in field studies, able
to drive and maintain vehicles and have experience of
estate work. In practice most successful candidates have at
least A-level standard in biology and many are graduates.

✍ **Further information** English Nature, Northminster
House, Peterborough PE1 1UA

▥ **Reading** *Working In* Series: *The Countryside* published
by and available from the Careers and Occupational
Information Centre, price £2.35

☛ School careers library classification WAR

Naval Architecture
see **Engineering**

Navy
see **Royal Navy and Royal Marines**

Neurophysiology Technology Work

A more familiar name for the neurophysiology
technologist is the EEG (electro-encephalography)
technologist, who is responsible for setting up and
operating electronic equipment which records the
electrical activity of the brain and nervous system.

☛ Two-year part-time day-release or block-release
course for the BTEC National Certificate in Science
(physiological measurement options) while working for a
hospital or a Regional Health Authority. Four GCSEs at
grades A, B or C are required including English,
mathematics and double award science. The National
Certificate may be followed by the BTEC Higher National

Certificate in Physiological Measurement.
✍ **Further information** Electro-Physiological
Technologists' Association (EPTA), Neurophysiology
Department, Selly Oak Hospital, Birmingham B29 6JD
▥ **Reading** *A Career in Clinical Neurophysiology*
published by and available free from EPTA
Medical Technical Officers and Assistants (HSC 13)
published by the Department of Health and available free
from Health Service Careers, PO Box 204, London
SE5 7ES

Nursery Nursing

Nursery nurses work with children under eight; they do
not generally nurse sick children although some find
employment in hospitals as play therapists. They work in
nursery schools and classes with children between the
ages of three and five, and in day nurseries, which take
children under five all day. They also work as nannies in
private households and in crèches attached to leisure centres
and further education colleges and in many other settings.
☛ Two-year full-time college course (as it is in a
modular format it can be taken part-time in up to five
years) with practical experience in an approved setting for
the Diploma or Preliminary Diploma in Nursery Nursing.
Students progress from the Preliminary Diploma to the
Diploma by completion of an intensive extra term or
part-time over a year. There are no nationally set entry
requirements but some colleges require two or more
GCSEs at grades A, B or C. Minimum age 16.
☛ Twenty-four month or longer full-time diploma course
at a private nursery training college, affiliated to the
Association of Nursery Training Colleges. Three GCSEs at
grades A, B or C including English are required.
Minimum age 18.
✍ **Further information** National Nursery Examination
Board, 8 Chequer Street, St Albans, Hertfordshire AL1 3XZ

⑪ Reading *Nursery Nursing* – a *Life with Children*
published by and available free from the National Nursery
Examination Board, please send a large stamped
addressed envelope
☛ School careers library classification KEC

Nursing

Nurses help to care for patients with mental and physical
disorders both in the community and in hospital.
☛ Three-year full-time registered general nurse training
in a hospital. A minimum of five GCSEs at grades A, B or
C is required. No particular subjects are specified;
however, most schools of nursing now require applicants
to have five academic GCSEs at grades A, B or C including
English and mathematics and/or single or double award
science. Very popular nurse training schools may require
A-levels. Minimum age 17½.
☛ A good base of GCSEs at grades A, B or C and at least
two A-levels are required for a four-year degree course in
nursing. A-levels in physics, chemistry and biology are
preferred; if these A-levels are not held, science GCSEs are
required. See Higher Education on page 132.
☛ Three-year full-time course in a college of nursing
which is linked to a college of higher education or a
university. Students will receive a non-means-tested
bursary and gain clinical experience in hospitals and in
the community. These new courses are known as Project
2000 and will run alongside the traditional training and
will eventually replace it. Entry qualifications are five
GCSEs at grades A, B or C.
✍ **Further information** Regional Health Authorities,
addresses in telephone directories
English National Board for Nursing, Midwifery and
Health visiting, Careers Advisory Service, PO Box 356,
Sheffield s8 osj
⑪ Reading *Registered General Nurse/Registered Mental*

Nurse/Registered Nurse for the Mentally Handicapped (HSC2) published by the Department of Health and available free from Health Service Careers, PO Box 204, London SE5 7ES

☛ School careers library classification JAD

Occupational Therapy

The occupational therapist's aim is to enable those who are temporarily or permanently disabled to be as independent as possible in their everyday lives, whilst recovering from illness or adapting to disability.

☛ Three-year full-time course at a recognised school attached to a hospital or university. Five GCSEs at grades A, B or C including English and at least one science subject and two academic A-levels are required.

✍ **Further information** College of Occupational Therapists, 6–8 Marshalsea Road, Southwark, London SE1 1HL

⩗ **Reading** *The Occupational Therapist* available free from the College of Occupational Therapists (please send a stamped addressed envelope)

☛ School careers library classification JAR

Operational Research

Operational researchers often use mathematical and computer-based models in helping decision-makers in industry, commerce, government and public service to solve complex problems, many of which entail a significant degree of risk or uncertainty.

☛ A degree with some mathematical or statistical study is essential; some degree courses include options in operational research. A good base of GCSEs at grades A, B or C including mathematics and A-levels in mathematics, science, social science or economics are required. See Higher Education on page 132.

✍ **Further information** Operational Research Society, Neville House, Waterloo Street, Birmingham B2 5TX

▥ **Reading** *A Career in Operational Research* published by and available free from the Operational Research Society

☛ School careers library classification PAJ

Optometry (ophthalmic optics)

Optometrists (ophthalmic opticians) test and examine eyes and prescribe spectacles and contact lenses.

☛ Three-year full-time degree course in optometry (ophthalmic optics) for which three GCSEs at grades A, B or C and generally three A-levels are required, two of which must be chemistry, mathematics, physics or biology. Subjects not held at A-level should be held at GCSE if possible.

✍ **Further information** The British College of Optometrists, 10 Knaresborough Place, London SW5 OTG

▥ **Reading** *A Career in Vision Care* published by and available free from the General Optical Council, 41 Harley Street, London W1N 2DJ

☛ School careers library classification JAL

Ordnance Survey Work
see **Cartography**

Organisation and Methods and Work Study

Work study officers study how work is done and suggest methods to improve efficiency. Organisation and methods officers apply the same techniques to office work.

☛ Full- or part-time course for Part I of the Diploma in Administrative Management of the Institute of Administrative Management. Four GCSEs at grades A, B or C including English and one A-level or an appropriate BTEC National is required for entry.

☛ Part-time, full-time or sandwich course for the BTEC National Certificate/Diploma in Business and Finance. Four GCSEs at grades A, B or C including English and mathematics are required. This may be followed by study for BTEC Higher National Certificates/Diplomas which may include options in work study or organisation and methods. The courses leading to the higher awards may also be entered with candidates with one A-level.

☛ One-year part-time study, distance learning or a short concentrated course for the Management Services Certificate of Competence. Ideally candidates should have several GCSEs including English and mathematics and one or more A-levels or a BTEC National in Business and Finance. Entry to management services is usually based on maturity and experience in handling people, and typically new entrants will have a degree or a BTEC Higher award. The Certificate can be followed by two-year part-time study for the Diploma in Project Management.

☛ A degree in any subject or an appropriate professional qualification, eg in banking or accountancy, followed by either on-the-job training or part-time study for the examinations of the professional institutes.

✍ **Further information** Institute of Administrative Management, 40 Chatsworth Parade, Petts Wood, Orpington, Kent BR5 1RW
Institute of Management Services, 1 Cecil Court, London Road, Enfield, Middlesex EN2 6DD

▥ **Reading** *Choosing a Career in Management Services* published by and available free from the Institute of Management Services

☛ School careers library classification PAG

Orthoptics

Orthoptists work as part of the eye-care team, diagnosing and treating defects of binocular vision, eg squints and disorders of eye muscle movements. A lot of the work is with children, in both hospitals and health centres, but more adult patients are being referred for assessment and treatment.

☛ Full-time three-year orthoptics degree course at Liverpool and Sheffield Universities and Queen's College, Glasgow. Five GCSEs at grades A, B or C including English, mathematics and preferably double award science and three A-levels, preferably including biology are normally required.

✍ **Further information** British Orthoptic Society, Tavistock House North, Tavistock Square, London WC1 9HX

▥ **Reading** *Orthoptist* (HSC16) published by the Department of Health and available free from Health Service Careers, PO Box 204, London SE5 7ES

☛ School careers library classification JAM

Osteopathy

Osteopaths treat people using their hands and pay particular attention to the effects that muscles and ligaments have on joint movement. Osteopaths do not work within the National Health Service.

☛ Four-year full-time course for which five GCSEs at grades A, B or C including English and two A-levels preferably in chemistry and biology are required. All GCSE subjects are acceptable. This course leads to the Degree in Osteopathy recognised by the General Council and Register of Osteopaths.

✍ **Further information** The British School of Osteopathy, 1/4 Suffolk Street, London SW1Y 4HG

▥ **Reading** Leaflet published by and available free from the British School of Osteopathy

☞ School careers library classification JOD

Painting and Decorating
see **Building Crafts**

Patents

Patent agents advise their clients on patent law: for example, whether a 'new' invention has already been patented and therefore is not really new. They do similar work with trademarks and industrial design. Their main work is drafting the description of the invention which forms the basis of the protection given by the patent. They operate in private practice or in large industrial firms. **Patent examiners** work in the Patent Office and examine applications for patents to ensure that only really 'new' inventions qualify for granted patents.

Patent Agents
☞ A degree course in science, applied science, mathematics or engineering is virtually essential. A good base of GCSEs at grades A, B or C for A-level specialisation in sciences and/or mathematics will be required for entry to a degree course. See Higher Education on page 132. The degree should be followed by three years' study for the Institute's examinations while working in a suitable office. After passing the Institute's examinations a patent agent will be able to work in this country, but to practise before the European Patent Office a further examination must be passed. It is possible to sit the Institute's examinations without a degree but nowadays very few people do so.

Patent Examiner
☞ A first or second class honours degree in science, engineering, mathematics or an equivalent professional qualification is required. On-the-job training is given. See Higher Education on page 132.

✍ **Further information** The Chartered Institute of Patent Agents, Staple Inn Buildings, High Holborn, London WC1V 7PZ
The Principal Examiner (Administration), The Patent Office, Concept House, Cardiff Road, Newport, Gwent NP9 1RH (for patent examiners)

📖 **Reading** *Patent Agency – a Career for You?* published by and available free from the Chartered Institute of Patent Agents
Patent Examiner – A Career as a Patent Examiner published by and available free from the Patent Office
☞ School careers library classification ROP

Personnel Work

Personnel managers recruit and select staff, run staff training programmes, negotiate with trades unions about pay and working conditions. They work in local authorities and hospitals as well as in commercial and industrial concerns.

☞ Part-time or full-time study for the examinations of the Institute of Personnel Management. To become a student member you will normally need to have three GCSEs at grades A, B or C and two A-levels, no subject to be counted at both levels, or to have passed the Certificate in Personnel Practice course. No academic qualifications are required to enter the one-year Certificate in Personnel Practice course.

☞ Part-time or full-time course for the BTEC Higher National Certificate/Diploma in Business and Finance; it is possible to take modules specialising in personnel work. Three GCSEs at grades A, B or C and one A-level or a BTEC National award is required for entry. This should be followed by study for the Institute's examinations. BTEC Higher award holders may be given exemptions.

☞ Degree in any subject followed either by a postgraduate course in personnel management and/or full-time or part-time study for the Institute's examinations. Accreditations towards the Institute's examinations may be granted to holders of certain postgraduate diplomas.

☛ Degree in human resource management, public administration or business studies followed by part-time or full-time study for the Institute's examinations. Accreditation may be granted towards the Institute's examinations for candidates with appropriate degrees. See Higher Education on page 132.

✍ **Further information** Institute of Personnel Management, IPM House, Camp Road, Wimbledon, London sw19 4ux

▥ **Reading** Leaflets are published and available free from the Institute

☛ School careers library classification CAS

Pharmacy

Pharmacists prepare medicines from natural and synthetic products and dispense them to the public. Most pharmacists work in community pharmacies (retail chemists' shops) and are involved not only in dispensing medicines and counselling patients on their proper use, but also in advising the public on a variety of health care issues. Hospital pharmacists, in addition to dispensing medicines, advise their medical and nursing colleagues on the effects of medicines and warn them of any toxic side-effects. Industrial pharmacists are involved in a wide variety of occupations, research, production, marketing, general administration and technical and medical information.

☛ A pharmacy degree and one-year's pre-registration training (ie paid practical training) are essential for registration as a pharmaceutical chemist. A good base of GCSEs at grades A, B or C and three A-levels, one of which must usually be chemistry, the others chosen from

physics, a mathematical subject and a biological subject,
are required. See Higher Education on page 132.

✍ **Further information** Royal Pharmaceutical Society of
Great Britain, 1 Lambeth High Street, London SE1 7JN

▥ **Reading** *Pharmacy and Pharmacology Degree Course
Guide* published by Hobsons Publishing PLC, price £5.95
Pharmacy: Effective Caring and *Entrance Requirements to
Schools of Pharmacy* published by and available free from
the Royal Pharmaceutical Society of Great Britain

☛ School careers library classification JAG

Pharmacy Technician Work
see **Dispensing Assistant**

Photography

Photographs are required for advertising, illustration,
portraits (especially at weddings), scientific and medical
work. Photographers may process the photographs
themselves or employ technicians to do this.

☛ Three-year part-time, one- to two-year full-time
courses for the City and Guilds Certificate No. 747
Professional Photography. Entry qualifications vary but
can be as high as three GCSEs at grades A, B or C.

☛ Full-time or part-time college courses for a BTEC
National Certificate/Diploma in Design (Photography) or
Photographic Technology. Four GCSEs at grades A, B or
C or a BTEC First Certificate/Diploma is required for
entry.

☛ Two-year full-time course for the BTEC Higher
National Diploma in Photography. A BTEC National
Certificate/Diploma with appropriate units or a
foundation course in art and design is required for entry.
Generally candidates straight from school should have
three GCSEs at grades A, B or C and two A-levels. Some
colleges specify certain GCSE subjects such as art, English,

mathematics and science. Some colleges will accept candidates with one A-level. In some colleges the two-year course can be followed by an additional year's course leading to the Professional Qualifying Examination of the British Institute of Professional Photography.

☛ Three-year full-time course for a degree in photography. A good base of GCSEs at grades A, B or C and two A-levels or a BTEC National Diploma or satisfactory completion of a foundation course in art and design together with five GCSEs at grades A, B or C or three GCSEs at grades A, B or C and one A-level.

For all the photography courses above most colleges also expect candidates to have a portfolio of work to show at the interview.

☛ Three-year full-time course for a degree in photographic sciences. Three GCSEs at grades A, B or C including chemistry, mathematics and physics and two A-levels including at least one of these subjects. A-levels in all three are preferred.

Press Photography

☛ One-year full-time course for press photographers. One A-level and four GCSEs at grades A, B or C including English are required. An 18-month qualifying period on a regional or local newspaper is required before sitting the National Certificate examination.

☛ Direct entry with five GCSEs at grades A, B or C including English or two years' photographic experience or after taking a further education course in photography. Training is by block release. A two-year qualifying period is required before sitting the National Certificate examination.

✍ **Further information** British Institute of Professional Photography, Fox Talbot House, 2 Amwell End, Ware, Hertfordshire SG12 9HN

Royal Photographic Society, The Octagon, Milsom Street, Bath BA1 1DN

For press photographers: Training Department, the Newspaper Society, Bloomsbury House, Bloomsbury Square, 74–77 Great Russell Street, London WC1B 3DA (please send a large stamped addressed envelope)

IIII Reading *Getting Jobs in Photography*, price £4.50 and *An Eye for the Job,* price 75 pence, both published by and available from the British Institute of Professional Photography

☛ School careers library classification EV

Physics

Physics is the study of matter and energy. Physicists apply their knowledge in fields as diverse as electronics, optics, acoustics and medical physics.

☛ If you are planning from the outset to be a professional physicist you should take a degree course in physics or applied physics at a university or college of higher education. A good base of GCSEs at grades A, B or C and specialisation in mathematics and physics at A-level will be required. See Higher Education on page 132.

☛ Two-year full-time or equivalent part-time course for the BTEC National Certificate/Diploma in Science. Four GCSEs at grades A, B or C including mathematics and a science subject or a BTEC First Certificate/Diploma is required for entry. The BTEC National awards can be followed by study for the BTEC Higher National Certificate or Higher National Diploma in Science (Physics) for which three GCSEs including mathematics, a subject testing command of English, A-level physics and mathematics studied beyond GCSE are alternative entry qualifications.

✍ **Further information** The Institute of Physics, 47 Belgrave Square, London SW1X 8QX

IIII Reading *Physics and Physicists, What is Physics?, What do Physicists Do?, Working in Physics* and *A Day in the Life* published by and available free from the

Education Department, the Institute of Physics
☛ School careers library classification QOF

Physiological Measurement
see **Cardiology Technician Work** *and*
Neurophysiology Technology Work

Physiotherapy

Physiotherapists work under the direction of a doctor
treating injuries and disease with exercises, massage and
electrotherapy.
☛ Three- or four-year full-time approved degree course
at a training school attached to a hospital or university. A
minimum of five GCSEs at grades A, B or C and two A-
levels preferably including biology are required. The
GCSEs must include English and double award science.
✍ **Further information** Chartered Society of
Physiotherapy, 14 Bedford Row, London WC1R 4ED
▥ **Reading** Leaflets published by and available from the
Society
☛ School careers library classification JAN

Piloting
see **Air Piloting**

Planning
see **Town Planning**

Plastering
see **Building Crafts**

Plastics and Rubber Technology and Engineering
see **Materials Science and Metallurgy**

Police and Security Services

The police maintain law and order by preventing and detecting crime. They work in traffic control, in the CID or with young people. Security officers work for private security firms guarding premises and transporting large amounts of cash from banks and other businesses.

Police

☞ Two-year on-the-job training includes courses at a training centre after passing an entrance examination. Four GCSEs at grades A, B or C including English and mathematics may give exemption from the entrance examination but most forces require all candidates to sit the entrance examination. All GCSE subjects are acceptable. Minimum age 18^1/$_2$. Candidates must be physically fit and meet the minimum height and eyesight standards.

☞ Cadet force entry is normally between 16 and 18^1/$_2$ years. Training combines educational studies, physical and adventure training together with community service and instruction in police work. Many forces prefer candidates with some GCSEs not necessarily at grade A, B or C.

☞ A degree in any subject plus selection tests for the Special Course leading to accelerated promotion. See Higher Education on page 132.

The Metropolitan Police of London recruit cadets nationwide but all other police forces recruit cadets from their force area only.

Security Officers

☞ Each firm lays down its own entrance requirements but preference is given to candidates with some GCSEs at grade E and above.

✍ **Further information** Police Recruiting Department, Home Office, 50 Queen Anne's Gate, London SW1H 9AT

📖 **Reading** *Working In* Series: *Police and Security*

published by and available from the Careers and
Occupational Information Centre, price £2.50
☛ School careers library classification MAB

Polymer Technology
see **Materials Science and Metallurgy**

Post Office Work

Post Office Counters
Counter Clerks work behind Post Office counters
carrying out many types of business transactions – selling
stamps and postal orders; accepting parcels; paying
pensions and allowances: dealing with National Girobank
and National Savings Bank accounts; issuing licences and
British visitors' passports.

Royal Mail
Letters administrators carry out office duties.
Postmen and **postwomen** collect, sort and deliver the
mail.
☛ For counter clerks the Post Office recruits people of a
good educational standard, eg four GCSEs including
English and mathematics. However, formal qualifications
are not essential as all applicants must pass an aptitude
test which measures the skills needed for the job. Those
successful in the test will be invited to interview.
☛ For postmen and women preference is normally given
to candidates with some GCSEs at grade E and above.
✍ **Further information** Local Divisional Personnel
Units
▥ **Reading** Leaflets published by the Post Office and
available free from your local Divisional Personnel Unit
☛ School careers library classification CAM

Poultry Farming
see **Farming**

Printing

Printing firms produce a wide range of printed material from the obvious books, newspapers and magazines to labels, wallpaper, cardboard boxes and plastic bags. Computers are an integral part of the modern printing process.

The work is prepared by craft-level workers in the printing preparation trades of planners, plate-makers, compositors, camera operators and scanner operators. Printing machine operatives in lithography, letterpress or photogravure who are skilled craft-level operatives run the printing presses. The work then passes to the Finishing Department, books are bound by hand or machine and the finishing machine operators fold, stitch and trim. Printing technologists or managers supervise the whole process. After discussion with the customer, they choose the most suitable paper and printing medium for the job, estimate the final cost and ensure a smooth workflow.

Printing Crafts

☛ Since 1983 the old apprenticeship system in printing has been replaced by a system where the length of training depends on the time needed to reach standards of competence. Recruits to most printing crafts are now called trainees; those in the print preparation trades are 'agreement trainees'. All trainees under 18 have to complete a college-based course the first term of which is usually full time, followed by periods of block-release study in the other five terms. Generally the courses lead to City and Guilds Certificates and a National Vocational Qualification. Most employers prefer candidates with GCSEs at grade D or above in English, mathematics, technology and double award science. For the print preparation trades good spelling and the ability to handle delicate materials such as film and photographic paper are essential. Machine operatives should also have good colour vision. In London and the South East there are regional selection tests including colour vision and intelligence tests followed by interviews. The British Printing Industries Federation then compiles a register of suitable candidates from which employers select trainees.

✍ **Further information** British Printing Industries Federation, 11 Bedford Row, London WC1R 4DX

▥ **Reading** A Careers Pack is published by and available free from the British Printing Industries Federation

☛ School careers library classification SAR

Printing Technology

☛ Full-time and part-time college courses for the BTEC National Diploma/Certificate in Printing. Four GCSEs at grades A, B or C, a BTEC First Certificate/Diploma or a City and Guilds Certificate is required for entry. The BTEC National awards can be followed by a BTEC Higher National Diploma/Certificate; these courses can also be entered with three GCSEs at grades A, B or C including mathematics and science and one appropriate A-level.

☛ Four-year sandwich course for a degree in printing technology. A good base of GCSEs at grades A, B or C including mathematics and at least two A-levels including one from chemistry, mathematics or physics are required. See Higher Education on page 132.

✍ **Further information** Institute of Printing, 8 Lonsdale Gardens, Tunbridge Wells, Kent TN1 1NU

☛ School careers library classification SAR

Typography

Courses leading to BTEC National Diploma/Certificates, Higher National Diplomas or degrees in art and design specialising in graphic design. See Art and design for details of entrance requirements.

✍ **Further information** Chartered Society of Designers, 29 Bedford Square, London WC1B 3GG

Society of Typographic Designers, New Inn Lane,

Avening, Tetbury, Gloucestershire GL8 8NB
☛ School careers library classification ED, or under
printing SAR

Prison Work

Prison officers are in charge of the day-to-day care of the
prisoners. Governors and assistant governors are in
overall charge of the prison, remand centre, youth
custody or detention centre.

☛ For prison officers: on-the-job training generally
lasting three months. The first month is spent at a nearby
prison or youth custody centre and the next two months
at a prison officers' training school. There are no specific
entry requirements but reasonable proficiency in reading,
writing, spelling and arithmetic is needed to pass the
aptitude test. Minimum age 21.

☛ Prison officers can be promoted to assistant governor.
For direct entry as an assistant governor there are no
specific educational requirements but in practice most
successful candidates for the accelerated promotion
scheme have degrees or equivalent qualifications.

✍ **Further information** The Recruiting Office, The
Home Office, (Prison Service), Cleland House, Page
Street, London SW1P 4LN

▥ **Reading** *The Inside Story* (prison officers), and *Inside
Management* (assistant governors) published by and
available free from the Home Office

☛ School careers library classification MAD

Producing
see **Drama, Film and Video Production** *and*
Broadcasting

Psychology

Psychologists should not be confused with psychiatrists,

who are doctors who treat the mentally ill. Psychologists study human behaviour and apply their knowledge in the fields of educational, clinical or occupational psychology. Educational psychologists work for local education authorities advising on children's emotional and behavioural problems and running the School Psychological Service. Clinical psychologists are employed in the NHS helping people with behavioural and emotional problems. Occupational psychologists are trained to help people adapt to their work environment. They also try to adjust the environment to the needs of those who work in it.

☛ A degree in psychology and postgraduate training is essential. A good base of GCSEs including mathematics and at least two A-levels are required. Some courses require science A-levels so it would be wise to have double award science among your GCSE subjects. See Higher Education on page 132.

✍ **Further information** The British Psychological Society, St Andrew's House, 48 Princess Road East, Leicester LE1 7DR

▥ **Reading** *How about Psychology* published by and available from the British Psychological Society, price £1.95 *Psychology Degree Course Guide* published by Hobsons Publishing PLC, price £5.95

☛ School careers library classification KEL

Public Health Inspection
see **Environmental Health**

Public Relations

A public relations officer's job, whether employed in house or as a consultant, is to promote the organisation he or she serves. This is done by preparing publications, organising exhibitions, answering queries from the public and liaising with the media.

☛ Full-time or part-time college courses for a BTEC National Certificate/Diploma in Business and Finance. Four GCSEs at grades A, B or C preferably including English and mathematics or a BTEC First Certificate/Diploma is required for entry. This can be followed by either a course for a BTEC Higher National Certificate/Diploma and by study for the CAM Certificate (see below).

☛ Two years' day-release or evening study for the Communication, Advertising and Marketing Education Foundation (CAM) Certificate in Communication Studies. The subjects studied are: marketing; advertising; public relations; media; research and behavioural studies; sales promotion and direct marketing. All students must be 18. They must have three GCSEs at grades A, B or C and two A-levels or five GCSEs and have been employed in a relevant field for one year of a BTEC National Certificate/Diploma in Business and Finance. All students must hold English GCSE at grades A, B or C. The CAM Diploma in Public Relations involves a further year's study. In addition students must have four years' experience.

☛ A degree in any subject. See Higher Education on page 132. Some degrees in business studies give exemptions from the CAM examinations. There are some degree courses which specialise in public relations. Most entrants to PR work are graduates. Fluency in speech and writing is essential. There is keen competition for vacancies. For membership of the Institute four years' experience is also required.

✍ **Further information** Institute of Public Relations, The Old Trading House, 15 Northburgh Street, London EC1V 0PR

▥ **Reading** *Public Relations as a Career* published by and available free from the Institute

☛ School careers library classification OG

Publishing

Publishers select or commission manuscripts from authors, and arrange for their printing. They organise the distribution and marketing of finished books.

☛ Virtually no editorial posts in publishing firms are open to school-leavers; experience as a publisher's representative or bookshop assistant can be a useful introduction to the marketing department of a publishing firm.

☛ Degree in any subject plus some specialised knowledge for editorial work. There are very few posts in editorial departments and competition is extremely fierce. See Higher Education on page 132. Some people enter editorial work after secretarial work in publishers' offices.

✍ **Further information** The Publishers' Association, 19 Bedford Square, London wc1b 3hj

▥ **Reading** *Careers in Book Publishing* published by and available free from the Publishers' Association (please send a stamped addressed envelope)

Working In Series: *Printing and Publishing* published by and available from the Careers and Occupational Information Centre, price £2.35

☛ School careers library classification FAD

Purchasing and Stock Control

Purchasing officers work for large organisations. Their task is to buy raw materials for manufacturing, goods which are to be resold and articles for use in the organisation ranging from large items of equipment to office stationery. As supplies are often bought in bulk, special terms are negotiated. They may also be responsible for stock control, the management of stores and the distribution of goods.

☛ Four or five years' part-time study for the Institute's examinations while working in a suitable post. Three GCSEs at grades A, B or C including English and mathematics or another quantitative subject and two A-levels are required. All subjects are acceptable. Very few entrants qualify this way; the majority take further or higher education.

☛ Full-time or part-time college course for a BTEC National Certificate/Diploma in Business and Finance. Four GCSEs at grades A, B or C preferably including English and mathematics or a BTEC First Certificate/Diploma is required. The BTEC National awards can be followed by BTEC Higher awards which may contain options in purchasing. Courses leading to BTEC Higher awards may also be entered with three GCSEs at grades A, B or C and one A-level. BTEC Higher awards should be followed by study for the Institute's examinations; some BTEC options will give some exemptions from the Institute's examinations.

☛ A degree in any subject followed by one or two years' part-time study for the Institute's examinations. Some exemptions can be granted from the Institute's examinations for candidates with a degree in business studies with suitable purchasing options. For some posts a degree in engineering or applied science is valuable. See Higher Education on page 132.

✍ **Further information** Institute of Purchasing and Supply, Easton House, Easton on the Hill, Stamford, Lincolnshire PE9 3NZ

▥ **Reading** *Purchasing and Supply: A Career worth thinking about* published by and available free from the Institute

☛ School careers library classification OP

Quantity Surveying
see **Surveying**

Quarrying

Quarrying is extracting stone, slate, marble, gravel and
sand from the surface by drilling, blasting, cutting, etc.
These materials are used for constructing buildings and
roads. People working in quarrying sometimes have
qualifications in engineering (see Engineering).

☞ Three-year sandwich course at Doncaster
Metropolitan Institute of Higher Education for the BTEC
Higher National Diploma for which three GCSEs at
grades A, B or C and one A-level are required. The A-level
must be either mathematics or physics, the other subject
having been studied to that level. The course can also be
entered by students holding a BTEC National
Certificate/Diploma in mining or engineering.

✍ **Further information** The Institute of Quarrying,
7 Regent Street, Nottingham NG1 5BY

☞ School careers library classification ROB

Radio
see **Broadcasting**

Radio Engineering
see **Broadcasting, Engineering** *and*
Merchant Navy

Radiography and Radiotherapy

Diagnostic radiographers and therapy radiographers
work under the direction of a doctor. The diagnostic

radiographer takes X-rays to help the doctor diagnose illness and injuries. The therapy radiographer treats patients using radiation.

☛ Three-year full-time course in either diagnostic radiography or therapeutic radiography at a recognised school or centre in a hospital or university. Candidates have to comply with normal university admission requirements: two A-levels and three GCSEs at grades A, B or C or three A-levels and one GCSE at grade A, B or C. Additionally candidates who have gained eight points with one A-level, ie at grade A or B, satisfy the minimum requirement of the College of Radiographers. Schools of Radiography set their own course requirements which are in practice higher. Your GCSEs should include English, mathematics and double award science.

✍ **Further information** College of Radiographers, 14 Upper Wimpole Street, London w1m 8bn

▥ **Reading** *Radiography* published by the Department of Health and available free from Health Service Careers, PO Box 204, London se5 7es

☛ School careers library classification JAP

Recreation Management

Recreation managers (also known as leisure or amenity managers) work for local authorities, commercial companies and voluntary bodies managing sports, recreation and leisure centres, swimming pools, urban and country parks, sports grounds and entertainment, cultural, arts and community centres.

☛ Part-time study for the examinations of the Institute of Leisure and Amenity Management (ILAM). There are four ILAM qualifications: to study for the First Award four GCSEs at grades A, B or C or a BTEC First award is required. All GCSE subjects are acceptable. Pre-entry requirements for the Certificate in Leisure Operations are two A-levels or a BTEC National award in Leisure Studies.

Pre-entry requirements for the Certificate in Leisure Management include Higher National awards in appropriate subjects and leisure related degree courses. Finally to enter the Diploma in Leisure Management either an ILAM Certificate must be held or certain degree and postgraduate qualifications. For each level certain other qualifications are acceptable – details from ILAM.

☛ Management training scheme for the Institute of Baths and Recreation Management which consists of four modules studied part-time at college or by correspondence. The minimum recommended entry level is four GCSEs including English and mathematics and one A-level or BTEC National Diploma/Certificate.

☛ A degree in any subject or a comparable qualification followed by a one-year postgraduate course. There are also degree courses in leisure and recreation studies and in arts administration. See Higher Education on page 132.

✍ **Further information** Institute of Leisure and Amenity Management (ILAM), Lower Basildon, Reading, Berkshire RG8 9NE

Institute of Baths and Recreation Management, Giffard House, 36/38 Sherrard Street, Melton Mowbray, Leicester LE13 1XJ

▥ **Reading** *Careers in the Leisure Industry* published by and available from ILAM

☛ School careers library classification GAJ

Religious Work

Christian Church Work

Ordained ministers preach the faith, conduct services and baptisms, weddings and funerals as well as providing a social service, visiting the ill and the bereaved. In addition to the ordained ministry there are other openings for full-time work in the church for both men and women. These include youth work, social work, missionary work and parish work for which a wide range of professional qualifications is required although there are, in some cases, denominational training courses. In the Roman Catholic and Anglican churches only men may at present be ordained as priests. In the Anglican Church women and men may be ordained as deacons or accredited lay workers.

☛ Those entering the ministry take a course at a theological or bible college. The length of the course and the qualifications required depend on the candidate's age and denomination. Many candidates have already taken a university degree course (see Higher Education on page 132) but candidates without higher education qualifications should still apply.

🖎 **Further information** The Vocations Officer, Advisory Board of Ministry, Church House, Great Smith Street, London SW1P 3NZ (Church of England)

Secretary for Ministry, The Baptist Union, Baptist House, 129 Broadway, PO Box 44, Didcot, Oxfordshire OX11 8RT

The Methodist Church, Division of Ministries, Room 509, 25 Marylebone Road, London NW1 5JR

The United Reformed Church, Ministerial Training Committee, 86 Tavistock Place, London WC1H 9RT

Diocesan Vocations Service (RC), 31 Moor Road, Headingley, Leeds LS6 4BG

For other religious faiths

please consult your local place of worship

☛ School careers library classification FAM

Residential Care
see **Social Work**

Retail and Wholesale Distribution

Over two million people work in distribution – in small shops, large department stores, in mail-order firms and in wholesalers. Most have contact with the customers but buyers, who purchase stocks, do not meet the public. There are jobs in retailing for people at all levels of educational attainment. Some sales assistants know little about the products they sell, but many have specialised knowledge acquired on the job and on special training courses. There are many careers in retailing that are not dealt with in this section – display work, which includes window dressing is under Art and design; also look at the sections on personnel work, purchasing and stock control and accountancy.

☛ One-year full-time or two-year part-time college courses for a BTEC First Certificate/Diploma in Distribution Studies. There are no formal entry requirements but colleges may prefer students with some GCSEs at grade E or above. Many 16 and 17 year-old school-leavers are entering retailing through Youth Training (YT). The BTEC First Certificate/Diploma may be part of the training scheme.

☛ Full-time and part-time college courses for a BTEC National Diploma/Certificate in Distribution Studies. Four GCSEs at grades A, B or C or a BTEC First Certificate is required for entry.

☛ Two-year part-time course for BTEC Higher National Certificate, two-year full-time, three-year sandwich or three-year part-time course for BTEC Higher National Diploma. Entry requirements are three GCSEs at grades A, B or C and one A-level or an appropriate BTEC National Certificate or Diploma.

☛ A degree in any subject followed by on-the-job training and specialised courses. See Higher Education on page 132. A degree in business studies (in some colleges you can take optional subjects in distribution) would be particularly relevant. One university has a degree course in licensed retailing and other colleges and universities have specialised degree courses.

There are many training schemes run by specialised bodies, eg for selling wines and spirits, jewellery or flowers.

✍ **Further information** Distributive Industries Training
Trust, 5 Bridge Street, Bishop's Stortford, Hertfordshire
CM23 2JU

▥ **Reading** *Working In* Series: *The Retail Industry*
published by and available from the Careers and
Occupational Information Centre, price £2.50
There's a Great Career in Store for You published by and
available free from the Distributive Industries Training
Trust

☛ School careers library classification OF

Royal Air Force

National defence is the main task of all branches of HM
Forces. There are many different professional posts in the
Royal Air Force apart from flying; these include
administration, catering and medicine.

Officers

☛ Five GCSEs at grades A, B or C including English and
mathematics and two A-levels at grade E or better are
required; the subjects must not overlap significantly in
content and only one may be non-academic. The age
limits for the General Duties (Flying) Branch are 17½–24
for pilots, 26 for navigators. The age limits for the
Administrative Branch, General Duties (Ground) Branch
(which includes air traffic control and fighter control
duties) are 17½–30.

☛ The RAF can sponsor students for sixth-form study
and on degree courses. See Higher Education on
page 132.

Airmen/Women

☛ Entry requirements for aircrew who fly as crew on
planes are three GCSEs at grades A, B or C including
mathematics and English and be aged between 17½–26
on entry. At least an elementary knowledge of science is
required.

☞ For ground trades there are various entry requirements. Age limits are usually 16¹/₂–39. Candidates for technician training require up to four GCSEs at grades A, B or C including mathematics and a physics-based science subject.

Women have equal pay and can be employed on the same duties as men with the exception of RAF Regiment, Fire and Aerial Erector. This may change in the next few years so that all careers in the RAF are open to women.

✍ **Further information** Local RAF Careers Information Office (look under 'Royal Air Force' in the telephone directory)

▥ **Reading** A range of booklets is published by the Ministry of Defence and available free from the RAF Careers Information Offices

☞ School careers library classification Officers BAL, Airmen/women BAM

Royal Navy and Royal Marines

The Royal Navy is concerned with defence while the Merchant Navy transports cargo and passengers around the world (see Merchant Navy).

Naval officers
Full career commissions: Seaman, Engineering (mechanical and electrical), Supply and Secretariat and Royal Marines

☞ The Scholarship scheme for A-level study is limited to seamen, aircrew and engineering entrants. Five GCSEs at grades A, B or C are required. Age limits 15–17.

☞ Naval College entry: five GCSEs at grades A, B or C and two A-levels are required for all entries. For Seamen and Supply and Secretariat, English and mathematics must be included. For Engineering the A-levels must be mathematics and physics and GCSE English is also required. Age limits 17–23.

☞ University/college of higher education cadetship entry: candidates must obtain a place on a degree course or be already taking a degree course. They are awarded for all branches except instructor.

☞ Graduate entry: candidates must also have GCSEs at grades A, B or C in English and mathematics. Age limit 26. Higher age limits for instructors, medical officers and dental officers. See Higher Education on page 132.

Short Career Commissions

Naval College entry:

☞ **Seaman**: five GCSEs at grades A, B or C required including English and mathematics. Age limits 17–26.

☞ **Engineering**: three GCSEs at grades A, B or C including English and two A-levels in mathematics and physics are required. A BTEC National Certificate/Diploma in subjects appropriate to further mechanical or electrical specialisation is an alternative entry qualification. Age limits 17–26.

☞ **Royal Marines**: A minimum of five GCSEs at grades A, B or C including English and mathematics are required. Age limits 17–23, 25 for graduates.

Instructor, Medical and Dental Officers and Chaplains

☞ A good base of GCSEs at grades A, B or C, A-levels and higher education are essential. See Teaching, Medicine, Dentistry and Religious work.

Ratings and Marines

☞ The majority of ratings must pass a selection test but do not need GCSE qualifications. There are a few exceptions to this general rule.

Women join the Navy on exactly the same terms as men. The Women's Royal Naval Service (WRNS) is an integral part of the Royal Navy.

✍ **Further information** The Director, Naval Recruiting, Old Admiralty Building, London sw1a 2be

▥ **Reading** A range of booklets is published by the Ministry of Defence and is available free from your local Royal Navy Careers Office

☞ School careers library classification Officers BAB, Ratings BAD

Rubber Technology

see **Materials Science and Metallurgy**

afety Work

Safety officers are employed by industrial and commercial organisations to check that safe systems of work are used, that accidents are reported and that the legal requirements are met.

Factory inspectors are civil servants who visit industrial premises to ensure that the provisions of the Health and Safety at Work Act are being complied with.

☞ Part-time courses for the examinations of the National Examination Board in Occupational Safety and Health which leads to membership of the Institution of Occupational Safety and Health.

☞ Two-year on-the-job training for candidates for the factory inspectorate who have a good base of GCSEs at grades A, B or C including mathematics and a degree, BTEC Higher National Diploma, an equivalent or higher qualification in science or technology and three years' practical experience in industry.

☞ Full-time course for a degree in occupational safety and health. Contact the Institution for full details.

✍ **Further information** Health and Safety Executive, Personnel Management (CSIA), St Hugh's House, Bootle, Merseyside

Institution of Occupational Safety and Health,

222 Uppingham Road, Leicester LE5 0QG
▥ Reading *Health and Safety at Work: Advice,
Investigation and Enforcement* published by and available
free from the Health and Safety Executive
☛ School careers library classification COT

Science
see **Biochemistry, Biology, Chemistry,
Laboratory Technician Work** *and* **Physics**

Sculpture
see **Art and Design**

Secretarial Work

Secretarial work covers a wide range of employment that
can be entered at almost every level of educational
attainment. **Copy typists** type texts from handwritten or
previously typed drafts; they may also do some filing.
Audio typists type material from pre-recorded tapes.
Shorthand typists take dictation in shorthand and type
out the text later. The amount of responsibility that a
secretary is given varies. Some do shorthand typing, filing
and make appointments whereas others may be able to
work more on their own initiative. They may answer some
letters themselves, prepare agendas and keep minutes of
meetings. **Bilingual secretaries** may do some translation
work. Being able to operate a word-processor is an additional
skill that is becoming increasingly important. A word-
processor is basically a keyboard – which looks very much
like a typewriter – attached to a monitor and a printer. The
text is displayed on the monitor so mistakes can be easily
corrected. The machine has a 'memory' so text can be stored
to be used many times perhaps with slight changes each time.
☛ Direct entry with GCSE subjects and some typing
skills. This will usually lead to posts as copy, audio or
shorthand typists and not to secretarial posts.

☞ Part-time or full-time course in shorthand and typing at a college of further education. GCSEs at grade E or above may be required. This will usually lead to posts as copy, audio or shorthand typists and not to secretarial posts.

☞ Full-time courses at colleges of further education that lead to posts as secretaries generally demand at least four GCSEs at grades A, B or C. Secretarial courses including foreign languages require GCSE or A-level language study.

☞ Two-year part-time course for the BTEC National Certificate or two-year full-time or three-year sandwich course for the BTEC National Diploma in Business and Finance taking secretarial options. It is possible to specialise in agricultural secretarial work. The majority of the work as a farm secretary involves accounts and figure work–to a greater degree than most other secretarial jobs. The BTEC courses give students wider knowledge of the business world and can also be used as an entry qualification for higher level courses. Four GCSEs at grades A, B or C preferably including English and mathematics (or a BTEC First award) are required for entry.

☞ Two-year part-time course for the BTEC Higher National Certificate or two-year full-time, three-year sandwich or three-year part-time course for the BTEC Higher National Diploma in Business and Finance. It is possible to specialise in personal/private secretarial work. Three GCSEs at grades A, B or C, one A-level or a BTEC National award are required for entry.

☞ A degree in any subject followed by a secretarial course designed for graduates. Some are specifically for graduates in foreign languages. See Higher Education on page 132.

☞ Two-year full-time course for the Diploma of the Association of Medical Secretaries. Four GCSEs at grades A, B or C including English are required. Special provision is made for A-level entry candidates who are expected to complete the course in one year.

☛ One-year full-time course for the National Certificate for Farm Secretaries. Three GCSEs at grades A, B or C including English and mathematics (or a subject demonstrating numeracy) are required. Minimum age 17.

☛ Many school-leavers are entering office work under the Youth Training (YT) Office Studies Scheme.

✍ **Further information** Association of Medical Secretaries, Practice Administrators and Receptionists, Tavistock House North, Tavistock Square, London WC1H 9LN

Institute of Agricultural Secretaries, NAC, Stoneleigh, Kenilworth, Warwickshire CV8 1LZ

▥ **Reading** *Working In* Series: *Offices* published by and available from the Careers and Occupational Information Centre, price £2.50

☛ School careers library classification CAT

Shipbroking

Shipbrokers act as intermediaries between shipowners and people who have cargo to be sent abroad by sea. They are paid commission by the shipowner. They also represent the shipowner while the ship is in port and may arrange matters such as customs formalities or the loading of cargo. They may also buy and sell ships on behalf of owners or manage ships for their owners.

☛ Part-time study at a college of further education or by a correspondence course for the Membership Examinations of the Institute of Chartered Shipbrokers. Normally two A-levels or their equivalent are required.

✍ **Further information** The Institute of Chartered Shipbrokers, 3 Gracechurch Street, London EC3

▥ **Reading** Leaflet published by and available free from the Institute

☛ School careers library classification YAS

Social Work

Social workers help people to adjust to their social and personal problems. They are employed by local authority social services departments, education authorities, the probation service and by many voluntary bodies. They work in area offices, and often visit families in their homes. They also work in residential homes, day centres, hospitals, child guidance clinics and prisons. They train to work with people of all ages and of all types.

Qualifying Training

☛ The Diploma in Social Work (DipSW) is a new social work qualification. It replaces the Certificate in Social Services (CSS) and the Certificate of Qualification in Social Work (CQSW). DipSW training can be college-based or employment-based. The DipSW can be taken as part of a DipHE, a degree or a postgraduate qualification. Applicants under 21 for DipSW programmes require a good base of GCSEs and two A-levels or the equivalent. Mature students do not require formal qualifications but must demonstrate their ability to study at an advanced level. All applicants are usually required to have had some voluntary or paid work experience in social services or a related field.

Non-qualifying Training

☛ Courses leading to CCETSW's Preliminary Certificate in Social Care (PCSC) are run for 16–19 year-olds in colleges of further education. The PCSC is not a qualification but the course offers students the chance to learn about social services work while continuing their general education. There are no formal entry requirements but colleges often ask for some GCSEs at grade E or above.

☛ Full-time or part-time college course for BTEC First Certificate/Diploma in Caring. There are no formal entry requirements but many colleges ask for some GCSEs at grade E or above. This can be followed by the BTEC

National Certificate/Diploma in Caring Services (Social Care) an alternative entry requirement for the BTEC National course is four GCSEs at grades A, B or C. A BTEC National award will often be accepted as an entry qualification for a DipSW programme.

✍ **Further information** Central Council for Education and Training in Social Work (CCETSW), Information Service, Derbyshire House, St Chad's Street, London WC1H 8AD

CCETSW Information Service, Block B, 2nd Floor, South Gate House, Wood Street, Cardiff CF1 1EW

▥ **Reading** *Working In* Series: *Social Work* published by and available from the Careers and Occupational Information Centre, price £2.50

☛ School careers library classification KEB

Speech and Language Therapy

A speech and language therapist is professionally qualified to identify, assess and treat communication disorders in children and adults. The speech and language therapist has to work closely with members of the medical, teaching, psychological and other caring professions. While most speech therapists work in hospitals and community clinics they may also be found in schools, special units and adult training centres.

☛ Three- or four-year full-time degree course. A good base of GCSEs at grades A, B or C including English, a foreign language, mathematics and double award science and at least two A-levels are normally required. Some institutions require biology at A-level. See Higher Education on page 132.

✍ **Further information** College of Speech and Language Therapists, 7 Bath Place, Rivington Street, London EC2A 3DR

☛ School careers library classification JAS

Stage Management
see **Drama**

Statistics

Statisticians collect and interpret numerical data.

☛ A professional statistician needs a degree in statistics or in mathematics with statistics options. Entry requirements for a three- or four-year full-time or sandwich degree are a good base of GCSEs at grades A, B or C and at least two A-levels including mathematics. Alternatively a first degree in mathematics, economics or some science disciplines can be followed by a postgraduate course in statistics. See Higher Education on page 132.

☛ Part-time courses for the examinations of the Institute of Statisticians. The minimum entry requirement is two GCSEs at grades A, B or C in mathematics and English; in practice most candidates have much higher entry qualifications. The final part of the Institute's examination is equivalent to an honours degree in statistics.

☛ Full-time or part-time study for the BTEC Higher National Certificate/Diploma in mathematics, statistics and computing. Three GCSEs at grades A, B or C and A-level mathematics or a BTEC National award with a sufficiently high mathematical content is required for entry. The Higher Award courses can be followed by study for examinations of the Institute of Statisticians.

✍ **Further information** The Institute of Statisticians, 43 St Peter's Square, Preston, Lancashire PR1 7BX

▥ **Reading** *Careers in Statistics* published by and available from the Institute of Statisticians, price £1.75
Statistics and Your Career published by and available free from the Royal Statistical Society, 25 Enford Street, London W1H 2BH

☛ School careers library classification QOG

Stock Exchange Work

The London Stock Exchange is the central market place
for securities: stocks and shares in public limited
companies and government securities known as 'gilts'.
Careers are either within the London Stock Exchange
itself or in one of its member firms which are all over the
UK and the Republic of Ireland.

☛ The traditional roles of jobber and broker have been
replaced by the broker/dealer. All broker/dealers must
now take examinations before being allowed to trade or
offer investment advice. There are no formal entry
qualifications but confidence in working with numbers
and good communication skills are vital. In practice
many entrants have received higher education.

✍ **Further information** Public Information, The London
Stock Exchange, Old Broad Street, London EC2N 1HP

📖 **Reading** *Working In* Series: *Money Business* published
by and available from the Careers and Occupational
Information Centre, price £2.50

☛ School careers library classification NAL

Surveying

Building Surveying

Building surveyors inspect buildings and make reports on
their structural condition. They can advise clients on the
suitability of a building for specific purposes, prepare
schemes for conversion or repair and advise on costs. This
job is often combined with estate agency or valuation –
see Estate agency, auctioneering and valuation.

☛ Part-time study for the examinations of the
Incorporated Association of Architects and Surveyors.
Three GCSEs at grades A, B or C and two A-levels are
required. Mathematics, an appropriate science subject
and a subject requiring the use of descriptive English
must be included at either level. A BTEC National

Certificate/Diploma in Construction or Surveying may be an alternative entry qualification.

☛ Part-time study for the examinations of the Architects and Surveyors Institute. The educational requirements are under review – details from the Faculty.

☛ Three-year full-time or four-year sandwich degree course in building surveying. Three GCSEs at grades A, B or C and two A-levels are required. English or English literature and mathematics must be passed at either level. These degree courses give various exemptions from the examinations of the professional bodies; details from the individual professional bodies. See Higher Education on page 132.

Agricultural Land Surveying and Land Agency

An agricultural surveyor inspects and values agricultural land, farm buildings and stock. Land agents manage farms and estates.

☛ Part-time study for the examinations of the Incorporated Association of Architects and Surveyors.

☛ Three- or four-year degree or diploma course in land economy or land management. A good base of GCSEs including mathematics and English and at least two A-levels are required; in some colleges preference is given to candidates with mathematics A-level. These courses give various exemptions from the examinations of the professional bodies; details from the individual professional bodies. See Higher Education on page 132.

Land Surveying

Land surveyors measure the land and all the physical features so that maps can be prepared. There is little demand for land surveyors in this country and most posts are overseas. See also Cartography.

☛ Part-time study for the examinations of the Incorporated Association of Architects and Surveyors (see above under Building Surveying).

☛ Three-year full-time degree course in surveying and mapping sciences or land surveying. A good base of GCSEs at grades A, B or C including English or English literature, mathematics and physics is required together with two A-levels in mathematics and either physics or geography. A BTEC Certificate/Diploma with a significant content of mathematics and physics is an alternative entry qualification. Approved degree courses will exempt candidates from the examinations of the Royal Institution of Chartered Surveyors.

Mining Surveying

Mining surveyors measure and prepare detailed plans of mine workings.

☛ Four-year sandwich degree (giving exemption from RICS examinations). Three GCSEs at grades A, B or C and two A-levels are required. English or English literature and mathematics must be passed at either level.

Quantity Surveying

Quantity surveyors work out the costing of a building project and are employed either in private practice or in firms of architects or civil engineers. Construction surveyors are quantity surveyors working for building firms. They are responsible for financial management, especially for the preparation of tenders that are submitted to clients to obtain work.

☛ Three-year full-time or four-year sandwich course for a degree in quantity surveying giving exemption from RICS examinations. A good base of GCSEs at grades A, B or C and at least two A-levels are required. See Higher Education on page 132.

☛ Part-time study for the examinations of the Construction Surveyors' Institute. Four GCSEs at grades A, B or C including mathematics, English and a science are preferred. Students should be in approved employment and/or following an approved full-time or part-time course.

✍ **Further information** The Royal Institution of
Chartered Surveyors, Surveyor Court, Westwood Way,
Coventry CV4 8JE
The Incorporated Association of Architects and
Surveyors, Jubilee House, Billing Brook Road, Weston
Favell, Northampton NN3 3NW
The Construction Surveyors' Institute, Wellington House,
203 Lordship Lane, London SE22 8HA
British Coal, Hobart House, Grosvenor Place, London
SW1X 7AE (mining surveying only)
Architects and Surveyors' Institute, 15 St Mary Street,
Chippenham, Wiltshire SN15 3JN
▥ **Reading** *Making Land, Property and Construction
Work* published by and available free from the Royal
Institution of Chartered Surveyors
☞ School careers library classification UM

Surveying Technician Work

A surveying technician works under the direction of a
chartered surveyor.
☞ Full-time or part-time course for the BTEC National
Certificate/Diploma in building studies, land
administration, agriculture or surveying. Four GCSEs at
grades A, B or C including mathematics, a subject testing
command of English and for building preferably double
award science are required. An alternative entry
requirement is BTEC First Certificate/Diploma in
construction for which there are no formal entry
requirements although some colleges may prefer
applicants with some GCSEs at grade E or above. The
BTEC National awards can be followed by a BTEC Higher
National Certificate/Diploma and by the Joint Royal
Institution of Chartered Surveyors/Society of Surveying
Technicians' Test of Competence.
✍ **Further information** Society of Surveying Technicians,
Drayton House, 30 Gordon Street, London WC1H 0BH

☛ School careers library classification UM

☛eaching

Teachers work in a variety of schools and colleges ranging from small nursery schools to large sixth-form colleges. Primary teachers cover most subjects while secondary teachers specialise.

☛ Four-year full-time Bachelor of Education (BEd) degree course at a college of higher education or university. Three A-levels and one GCSE at grades A, B or C or two A-levels and three GCSEs at grades A, B or C are the normal minimum entry requirements. These passes must include English, science and mathematics at either level. Students may opt to train to teach lower or upper primary school children or a limited range of subjects in secondary schools.

☛ A degree and a one-year college-based postgraduate education course. All students must normally have GCSEs at grades A, B or C in English, mathematics and single award science.

☛ **Articled Teachers' Scheme** started in September 1990. Articled teachers are graduates and are school based spending two years training for the Postgraduate Certificate of Education.

☛ **Licensed Teachers' Scheme:** entrants must be over 26; hold GCSEs at grades A, B or C in English, mathematics and single award science and have undertaken a higher education course lasting two years full-time or the equivalent part-time (eg DipHE, BTEC HND/HNC) for the two-year school-based training.

Teaching Disabled Children

For teaching deaf, blind, physically or mentally disabled children the ordinary course (see above) should be taken. An additional course in teaching disabled children is taken after gaining some teaching experience. It is necessary before teaching blind or deaf children and recommended before teaching other disabled children.

✍ **Further information** Teaching as a Career (TASC), Department for Education, Sanctuary Buildings, Great Smith Street, Westminster, London SW1P 3BT

▥ **Reading** *A Career in Teaching* published by and available free from the Department for Education
The NATFHE Handbook of Initial Teacher Training copies of which can be found in most libraries and careers offices
☞ School careers library classification FAB

Textile Technology

Textile technologists apply their scientific knowledge to the manufacture and use of fibre, yarns and fabrics for the production of clothing, furnishings and carpets (see also Dyeing).

☞ Full-time or part-time college courses for a BTEC National Certificate/Diploma in Textiles. Four GCSEs at grades A, B or C or a BTEC First Certificate/Diploma is required. The BTEC National awards can be followed by study for the BTEC Higher National Certificate/Diploma in textiles and study for the Textile Institute's examinations. The BTEC Higher award courses can also be entered after sixth-form study. Three GCSEs at grades A, B or C including mathematics, a physical science and a subject testing the use of English and one A-level is required.

☞ Full-time or part-time study for the Textile Institute's Associateship Examinations at recognised centres. Five GCSEs at grades A, B or C including mathematics and two science subjects together with one A-level in any subject are required. All GCSE subjects are acceptable.

☞ Three- to four-year degree course in textiles or in a relevant subject such as chemistry, and a one-year postgraduate diploma. A good base of GCSEs at grades A, B or C and at least two A-levels is required. For courses in textile design or textile management the A-levels can be in any subject; GCSEs in art, mathematics, physics and chemistry are preferred. For courses in textile chemistry, A-levels in chemistry and physics are required and A-level mathematics is preferred. See Higher Education on page 132.

✍ **Further information** The Textile Institute, 10 Blackfriars Street, Manchester M3 5DR

☛ School careers library classification SAG

Tourism
see **Travel and Tourism Work**

Town Planning

Most planners work for local authorities drawing up broad plans for development, allocating areas for residential use, industrial use and open space. All future development and redevelopment must accord with these plans. Developers submit planning applications and planning permission is either granted or refused. Increasing numbers of planners are employed in the private sector.

Professional Planners

☛ Four-year full-time, five-year sandwich or six-year part-time undergraduate courses for a degree or diploma in planning, giving exemption from the Final Examination of the Royal Town Planning Institute. At least three GCSEs including English, mathematics and either history, geography or a language other than English and two A-levels are recommended. Some colleges require A-level mathematics and some require a science or geography or economics.

☛ Degree in any subject although degrees in related subjects such as economics, geography or law are sometimes preferred, followed by a two-year full-time or three-year part-time postgraduate course. See Higher Education on page 132.

Planning Technicians

☛ Part-time or full-time college course for a BTEC Certificate/Diploma in Land Use. Four GCSEs at grades A, B or C including mathematics and a subject testing use of English or a BTEC First Certificate/Diploma is required for entry. This can be followed by BTEC Higher National Certificates/Diplomas. These courses can also be entered after sixth-form study, four GCSEs at grades A, B or C including English and mathematics and one A-level is required for entry. Holders of these higher awards can become Members of the Society of Town Planning Technicians provided they also have four years' practical experience.

✍ **Further information** The Royal Town Planning Institute, 26 Portland Place, London WIN 4BE
The Society of Town Planning Technicians, at the same address

▥ **Reading** *Careers in Town Planning* and *General Information about Membership* published by and available free from the Royal Town Planning Institute
A Career as a Town Planning Technician for School Leavers published by and available from the Society of Town Planning Technicians

☛ School careers library classification US

Trading Standards Administration

Trading standards officers (sometimes called Consumer Protection Officers) enforce the wide range of legislation promoting and protecting fair and safe trading practices, such as the Trade Descriptions Act, the Weights and Measures Act and the Consumer Protection Act. They also advise and help members of the public, traders and business executives on trading issues and in some areas also get involved in a much wider range of duties, such as consumer education and enforcing animal health laws.

☛ Three-year block-release course for the Diploma in Trading Standards whilst working for a local authority. Three GCSEs at grades A, B or C and two A-levels are required including English, mathematics and physics at either level. Some of the candidates are graduates in any subject.

☛ Consumer advice officers take the Diploma in Consumer Affairs for which five GCSEs at grades A, B or C are required including English.

✍ **Further information** The Institute of Trading Standards Administration, Suite 18, Thamesgate House, 37 Victoria Avenue, Southend-on-Sea SS2 6BU

Local Government Management Board, Arndale House, Arndale Centre, Luton LU1 2TS

▥ **Reading** *A Career as a Trading Standards Officer* published by and available free from the Institute of Trading Standards Administration

☛ School careers library classification COP

Traffic Warden

Traffic wardens work under the direction of the police to ensure a smooth flow of traffic. They check that parking regulations are complied with and head school crossing patrols.

☛ On-the-job training in traffic warden work. There are no formal entry qualifications. Minimum age 18; successful candidates are usually older than 18.

✍ **Further information** Local Chief Constable – the address will be in the local telephone directory

☛ School careers library classification MAZ

Travel and Tourism Work

Travel agents arrange holidays and business travel for the public. They sell air, coach and train tickets and make hotel bookings and sell holidays arranged by the tour operators. Tour operators organise complete holidays at competitive prices.

☛ The ABTA NTB Youth Training Programme (YT) is for 16/17 year-olds. The programme will help you to achieve the Certificate in Travel Skills and the Diploma in Travel Skills. These are National Vocational Qualifications at Levels 2 and 3. As well as these Retail Travel qualifications there are also openings and qualifications available in business travel, tour operating and airlines. You can only join the Programme as a trainee employed in the travel industry. There are no formal entry requirements, but successful applicants often have three or four GCSEs at grades A, B or C. Selection concentrates on the appearance, enthusiasm, personality and common sense of the candidate. A flexible approach to work is also important.

☛ Full-time or part-time college courses for a BTEC National Certificate/Diploma in Business and Finance (Travel and Tourism). Four GCSEs at grades A, B or C or a BTEC First Award with credit is required for entry. There are no formal entry requirements for the BTEC First Award. The BTEC National awards can be followed by study for the BTEC Higher National Certificate/Diploma in Business and Finance with travel and tourism options. These courses can also be entered with three GCSEs at grades A, B or C and one A-level. Holders of the BTEC Higher National Diploma in Business and Finance with appropriate options gained at a college approved by the Institute are eligible to become full members of the Institute of Travel and Tourism.

☛ Degree course in tourism at some universities and colleges of higher education. It is also possible to take a degree in any subject and follow it with a postgraduate course in tourism.

✍ **Further information** The Institute of Travel and Tourism, 113 Victoria Street, St Albans, Hertfordshire AL1 3TJ (please send a stamped addressed envelope and £3 to cover costs)

Association of British Travel Agents National Training
Board (ABTA NTB), Waterloo house, 11–17 Chertsey
Road, Woking, Surrey HU21 5AL (a large stamped
addressed envelope must be enclosed)

▥ Reading *Working In* Series: *Travel and Tourism*
published by and available from the Careers and
Occupational Information Centre, both priced £2.35
The Handbook of Tourism and Leisure published by
Hobsons Publishing PLC, price £6.50

☞ School careers library classification YAP

Typography
see **Printing**

aluation
see **Estate Agency, Auctioneering and Valuation**

Veterinary Nursing

Veterinary nurses, formerly called animal nursing
auxiliaries, help veterinary surgeons treat animal illnesses
and accidents.

☞ Four GCSEs at grades A, B or C including English and
a single award science (preferably double award science)
or mathematics are required for enrolment as a trainee
under a scheme administered by the Royal College of
Veterinary Surgeons. All subjects are acceptable.
Minimum age 17. Two years' full-time gainful
employment in an approved veterinary practice or centre
and successful completion of preliminary and final
examinations are required for admission to the List of
Veterinary Nurses. Full-time courses may be attended for
up to six months of the two-year training period. It is not
possible for a veterinary nurse to become a veterinary
surgeon.

✍ **Further information** The British Veterinary Nursing Association, The Seedbed Centre, Coldharbour Rd, Harlow, Essex CM19 5AF

▥ **Reading** Free leaflet and Guide to the Scheme published by the Association, price £4.00 including postage

Working In Series: *Animals – Work With* published by and available from the Careers and Occupational Information Centre, price £2.65

☛ School careers library classification WAL

Veterinary Work

Veterinary surgeons, commonly known as 'vets', treat sick and injured animals. In the towns the animals would be household pets while a country vet treats mainly farm animals.

☛ Five- or six-year degree course in veterinary science. A good base of GCSEs at grades A, B or C including mathematics and double award science and three A-levels are required for entry. Generally the A-level requirements are biology, zoology, chemistry and either physics or mathematics.

✍ **Further information** Royal College of Veterinary Surgeons, 32 Belgrave Square, London SW1X 8QP

▥ **Reading** A free leaflet and *A Career as a Veterinary Surgeon* published by the Royal College of Veterinary Surgeons, price £4.00 post free

Veterinary Sciences Degree Course Guide published by Hobsons Publishing PLC, price £5.95

☛ School careers library classification WAL

Weights and Measures Inspection

see **Trading Standards Administration**

Wholesaling
see **Retail**

Word-Processing
see **Secretarial Work**

Youth and Community Work

Youth workers help young people to run clubs and other youth organisations. Community workers do similar work for people of all ages and take on the role of organiser, counsellor and welfare officer at a community centre.

☛ Two-year full-time diploma or certificate course for youth workers and/or community centre wardens. Five GCSEs at grades A, B or C will normally be required. Minimum age is generally 23.

☛ A good base of GCSEs at grades A, B or C and at least two A-levels are required for a degree in any subject followed by a one-year full-time postgraduate training course.

✍ **Further information** Council for Education and Training in Youth and Community Work, Wellington House, Wellington Street, Leicester LE1 6GD

▥ **Reading** *Initial Training Courses in Youth and Community Work* published by and available from the Council for Education and Training in Youth and Community Work, price £1

☛ School careers library classification KEG

Zookeeping

Zookeepers care for animals in zoos and safari parks. See also Veterinary nursing work.

☛ On-the-job training for animal keepers together with

a correspondence course (National Extension College) for
City and Guilds examinations. Formal educational
qualifications are not usually essential, but preference is
often given to candidates with some GCSEs at grade E or
above in biological subjects, English and mathematics.

☛ A degree in zoology. A good base of GCSEs at grades
A, B or C and at least two A-levels in biology, chemistry
and either physics or mathematics are generally required,
and if these subjects are not held at A-level they should be
held at GCSE. See Higher Education on page 132. There
are limited opportunities for professional zoologists in
zoos but other posts are open to them.

✍ **Further information** Zoological Society of London,
Regent's Park, London NW1 4RY and local zoos

▥ **Reading** *Careers in Zoology* and *Zookeeping* both
published by and available from the Zoological Society of
London

Working In Series: *Animals – Work With* published by and
available from the Careers and Occupational Information
Centre, price £2.65

☛ School careers library classification WAM

STUDENT HELPBOOK SERIES

This series of advice publications is designed to help students of all ages make the right choices about their careers and education. The books' animated text and cartoons make them a lively read for students who want to take their own decisions. Many careers teachers, advisers and parents find them an invaluable source of reference. The titles marked with an asterisk have been recommended by the Department of Employment for its Careers Library Initiative, a scheme designed to provide schools and colleges with first-rate careers information.

Titles in the series include:

- A Year Off ... A Year On?
- Decisions at 13/14+*
- Decisions at 15/16+*
- Decisions at 17/18+*
- Your Choice of A-levels
- Jobs and Careers after A-levels*
- Matters of Degree
- Hard Cash!

If you would like to order any of these titles, please contact Biblios Publishers' Distribution Services, Star Road, Partridge Green, West Sussex RH13 8LD (tel: 0403 710851).

For general information contact our Customer Services Department, Hobsons Publishing PLC, Bateman Street, Cambridge CB2 1LZ (tel: 0223 354551).